APPRECIABLE GIFTS

by

Sammy O. Joseph

Pulse Publishing House

Published in the United Kingdom by
Pulse Publishing House
Box 15129
Birmingham
England
B45 5DJ
pulsepublishinghouse@harvestways.org

Cover design and typesetting by Pulse Publishing House, England.

Printed in England.

ISBN 978-0-9567298-3-5

Contents

Acknowledgement   iv

Dedication   vi

Introduction   8

1   The Greatest Gift of All   11

2   The Gift of Restoration   27

3   The Gift of a True Friendship   37

4   The Gift of Sex and Sexuality
       in Committed Relationships   100

5   Cultivating the Gifts of
       Thanksgiving and Gratitude   155

References   178

Acknowledgement

I feel a great sense of both, awe and gratitude to the heavenly Father for surrounding me with such a great, qualified team of professional friends; the likes of Mark Golden, Suzie Tatnell, Bryn Davies and Dr. Joe "Cool" Ibanga. Their pieces of helpful advice and suggestions taken into prayerful and careful consideration have resulted into the production of what I describe as my best work, thus far!

How fortunate I am!

PULSE Publishing House and I would love to thank Sainsburys Plc. Northfield, England, through their Public Relations Manager, Debee Bowyer for facilitating us appreciable goodwill in the bureaucratic processes of organizing local press coverage for the book's launching!

Mark's critique awoke a fresh zeal in Pulse Publishing House to search farther, collective opinions from which this winning book-cover emerged, one which aptly interprets and summarizes the entire book! To all of you whose overwhelming vote carried the day, I say thank you! Dr. Joe "Cool" did a "cool" job, rummaging through the lines, proofreading repeatedly the manuscript, before Suzie and her team of designers ensured the delivery of an extremely fine, faultless, compact final package!

My characteristic late night calls brainstorming ideas – as

on past projects – gracefully eluded Bryn, our "in house" graphic consultant, having recently turned a doting father! However, your counsel and friendship are highly valued and appreciated, my friend!

To all of you not specifically mentioned by name, you are all very dear to me in friendship!

Thank you!

Dedication

I dedicate this work to all my friends right across the world whose influences upon me over the many years of formation, development and growth in spiritual matters have helped shaped my understanding of what rich rewarding friendships entails. Your "considerateness", each, has further enhanced me in the ministry to which I have been called.

Besides, I know it sounds strange to the ears to say that I have five equally best friends; nevertheless, it is true! Therefore, I honor these five people who constitute my inner-circle friends. These who, know me far beyond the veneer only afforded outside affiliates yet accept and love me, just for who I am: my darling Gabriella, David, Daniel, Priscilla and Paul, "the apostle". I am most grateful for your friendship, each. You opened my eyes wide to the very basic secrets of what true friendship entails.

To the friends and partners of *Sammy Joseph Ministries*, my spiritual sons and daughters – inclusive of those under the umbrella of *The Harvestways Int'l Church*, I thank you dearly, for entrusting me with your very hearts as a servant-pastor and a spiritual influence, upon your *very* souls!

Those whom I have successfully counseled – and it had led to happy conclusions, thank you too. Thank you for affording me the great honor and privilege to escort you some distance of your journeys in eternity! In every way, the lessons shared and stories retold on these pages are *not* entirely mine; they are *yours* – and *ours!*

Introduction

This book project affords you a great rare opportunity to read five books within *just* one, *Appreciable Gifts!*

Apart from the first couple of chapters that follow a chronological format, the subsequent three chapters are each, a separate piece! *Appreciable Gifts*, therefore, guarantees you the opportunity to commence reading, from any of its five chapters.

In such a day and an age when true and sincere gifts are rare – *rarely* offered, *rarely* exchanged and *rarely* received, you will find appreciable hints within the pages of this book that will sincerely guide you on the parameters of offering, accepting, cherishing, maintaining gifts – and abounding in them!

If you're seeking an inner peace and a deep-seated satisfaction in your friendships/relationships that have proven elusive, an inner healing from brokenness or an eternal friendship no other mundane friendship-type can afford to offer, search no further. Within the pages of *Appreciable Gifts* you will find your missing trophies!

The book is written in a direct, factual, reader-friendly way! I have attempted to approach the subject of "gifts" from an eternal perspective – not exclusively limited alone to the current mundane, physical existence in which we live.

As stated on the *Contents* page, each chapter addresses "different gifts", such as: the *Greatest Gift of All*, the *Gift of Restoration*, the *Gift of an Enduring Friendship*, the *Gift of Sex and Sexuality*, and finally; *Cultivating the Gifts of Gratitude and Thanksgiving!*

I do hope that you have a blessed reading!

Sammy Joseph
Birmingham
England.

If you are seeking an inner healing from 'brokenness', an eternal friendship no other mundane friendship-type can ever offer, or that inner peace that has proven elusive, search no further. Seek within the pages of *'The Greatest Gift of All'*; you will meet your very need!

"I have called you friends and not slaves ..."
Jesus Christ

"Behold what manner of love the Father has bestowed upon us, that we should be called the sons of God."
Apostle John

Chapter 1

The Greatest Gift of All

"For God so loved the world that He gave His only begotten Son, that whosoever believeth in him should not perish, but have everlasting life.

For God sent not His Son into the world to condemn the world; but that the world through him might be saved."
John 3:16-17

You have been there, so have I. We have suffered its effects. Everyone on the face of the planet has been heartbroken, at one time or another.

My experience of a broken heart had first occurred when I was a teenager. More precisely when I was fourteen! At that time, it had left me devastated. My parents had lost Joan – the eldest daughter in a close-knit family of two parents and four children!

Joan was my sister. But she was also my friend. She was twenty-two. I'd grieved, uncontrollably at hearing the news of her death. Ten months earlier, she had been happily married to a handsome University graduate, Johnson, in a publicized wedding ceremony. Shortly thereafter, their union had been blessed with a conception! Families from both sides looked forward to an addition to the clans.

However, it was never to be; the baby boy was excessively big for the canal. A late decision to have a *Cesarean*, coupled with some complications earlier undetected, terminated abruptly, both the lives of mother and infant son.

Both families were grief-stricken!

I do not remember about any other as I write, but my grief didn't last a month! I do remember, however, mourning for seven days wherein no morsel I had put onto my lips had been gracefully received by my taste buds; let alone my tummy. I had survived, only, on liquid!

Dad and mom had been very concerned for me, amidst their tears and grief. I assured them that it was my tribute to *my* Joan – and that I would be well.

Earlier, as a younger boy, I had grown in my walk with the Lord and obediently learned to forego food – in the art of waiting upon the Lord {fasting and praying coupled with reading and studying the scriptures} – usually on Saturdays. What I had *not* realized at the time was that God was going to use my grieving, to turn a new page initiating me into yet another dimension of walking with Him, for the rest of my life!

Individuals grieve very differently – and ought to, in measure!

By the end of July, however, God in His mercy had provided me a soothing comfort in a new female; a friend who was three months younger than I. We had met while my family holidayed at my Uncle's – away from the press of sympathizers who, daily, had thronged into our family home, with condolences. Strong bonds were quickly formed between my new friend and I.

At first, I referred to her as my "heaven-sent sister." However, our friendship grew, and blossomed. She became my first-ever girlfriend – *my first-ever love!*

Everyone saw a bright future in *us*. Everyone believed in *us*. *We believed in ourselves!*

Then arrived five months later, the negotiating of a turn – one of those crucial, uncontrollable curves that forever shape lives and destinies! My family was set to relocate from my Uncle's, to the farthest end of the city – and my girlfriend wasn't taking kindly to this new development. In those days of purity and innocence of love – don't misunderstand me, there still exists pure and innocent loves – and with teardrops welling up in her dark brown eyes which soon cascaded as a caress on those rotund cheeks, she confided in me, these very words: *"This is no joke, is it?"*

That was towards the end of the first academic term of 1982; the days when there was none of today's instant social communication methods: *BB-messaging, Mobile-texting, Facebooking, Tweeter or Computer e-mails!* Mobile phones did not exist and a working landline was the dream of sheer opulence!

In those days, the closest method of communication comparable to today's text was the telegram. But you never could afford it! Infact, almost everyone couldn't use the telegram; it was so expensive – yet sparse of words. You were allowed to send just a few counted words per time, only!

Huge companies made use of the *telegram* only if they had to relay important alerts to their branches, nationwide. The masses had *just* the Postal Agencies to rely upon for delivery of communication.

You would pop your stamped envelopes, air-mail letters or cards into the rectangular window atop the red cylindrical, five-foot high iconic *ER* post-boxes, erected outside the *Agency!* And B-I-N-G-O; off went your post! An alternative to the *ER* post box was a walking exercise to the *Agency* where you met with a lone staff – to whom you handed your business. By this time, I had made friends with the staff in here because I had become a *regular!*

At first, correspondence between *the lovebirds* was at par! We exchanged multiple pages of our futuristic expectations, gossips about our other friends and many other *tidbits* teenaged lovers loved to talk about, scribbled in ink. Additionally, most times, rouge lip-smacks that had been 'stolen' from her mom had embossed *my* sheets!

Those letters arrived every other week, which was fastest and most ideal. I ensured they were promptly read and replied – in the midnight hours. (One particular night, Dad had stumbled upon me replying one of her "love letters" at 3 *a.m.* And, oh, what a night that was!)

Then correspondence reduced to half-fortnightly; this frequency transpired for a quarter of a year! Before long, your guess would be as good as mine: communication gradually petered out! The handwriting on the wall was *very* legible, but I couldn't read the font in which they were written. I could only *do* bold, capital letters: I did *not* want another 'sister' taken away from me! But *my* second tragedy, barely a year apart, was already catching up on my heels! My heartthrob jilted me! She had 'fallen' for a mutual, age-mate friend of ours. Ouch; what a pain!

I *had* felt betrayed.

It had taken me quite a while to accept, overcome and heal from the subsequent negative feelings I had experienced!

Broken

Brokenness results from negative feelings and emotions.

Your brokenness may or may not be similar to mine. You may have become 'broken' as a result of an unforeseen mishap, an expectation unmet, a promise unfulfilled or a rejection from close-quarter that had led to your disillusionment! Hundreds, daily, become 'broken' by the sudden sprouting of an illness, the doctor's diagnosis or the bereavement/loss of a very dearly loved one. Their sad untimely departure has left others – including you – a huge void an enormous weight of daily responsibilities and chores. You currently barely exist in a dreamland!

Of no lesser significance, your life-long pet may have

suddenly taken ill, irrecoverably, and have had to be put down. The love of your life could just have announced to you, they needed *their* space – and a time of separation! Probably, the marriage you so much savored to save may just officially have altogether become dead; you stare into the noonday's sky in disbelief!

A further brokenness could arise due to the loss of a promising career or a sudden job lay-off – thus signaling a loss of earnings and financial security. A *"night of pleasure"* has materialized your fears and bitterness; it is confirmed: you've taken in.[1]

When life's issues negotiate you an unexpected turn, *two* basic reactions common to all anguish-types such as epitomized above are fear and deep anger. Soon, a number of negative emotions closely accompany these; such emotions as torment and despair, to mention just a couple. In most people, you won't find wanting the presence of deep depression coupled with self-harm, suicidal intents, resentment and confusion.

Resentment is a subtle aggrieved, bitter, hateful reaction accompanied by feelings of despondency, despair and frustration. It is the chief culprit often responsible for a hurting head and an aching heart. If left to fester, resentment could lead to a sudden outward outburst of a destructive anger; if contained within, to an inner physical, psychological or emotional wound.

The Creator-Father's Broken Heart
Some of us have even re-directed our resentment

against the Creator, Father-God! This only points to a universal fact: from whichever angle you cast your shots, brokenness necessarily requires healings! Quite obviously, all of humanity – and creation – are a broken piece! **Take it a notch further; even the Creator God's heart had also suffered some brokenness!**

Not a few times, scriptures record God's *'brokenness'* using such phrases as *"it grieved God and made him regretful"*, *"it displeased the Lord"*, *"it repented the Lord"* or *"it grieved him at his heart."*[2] Take for instance when our fore-parents – Adam and Eve – had disobeyed God in the Garden of Eden and had voted to succumb to the enticing temptation dangled under their noses by the serpent, the devil, Father God's heart had been broken! He had felt betrayed and rejected by His ace-creation: Man.

The authority and power to rule and dominate all elements on the earth which He (God) had bestowed upon Adam had been freely surrendered to the evil one.[3] Man had lost it forever. At least, so it seemed!

The effect of their foolishness had translated that thenceforth, both species of humankind – male and female – would be forever plagued. They had played into the hands of the wicked one. Willingly, they had opened the door to *"the thief"* and *"the robber"* to be plundered.[4] Strange occurrences un-intended by the Creator Father and Friend would roam, rule and reign in terror, over the domains of human existence. Sicknesses, illnesses, afflictions and death had come to pitch tents on Man's eternal, hitherto goodly heritage. Those evils wouldn't be evicted from their squatting position – at least, *not* without a stiff fight.

Why?

Because it was Man who had acquiesced the devils a legal license to stay *"lords of the land."* Man would toil – and his toil *may* never yield its optimum. Death, distress and diseases will begin to ravage humanity at will. Feuds and disagreements festered by jealousy, envy, greed and strife which started as little flicks of fire within friendly, familial, communal, and national settings would carry the potentials to erupt into large-scale fireballs! None of these was the friendly Creator-Father's intent for our world.

Adam's foolish treachery had deeply angered the Lord God – yet, He had the right to be angry!

More Brokenness: the Curse

Apart from Adam and Eve's betrayal of the Creator Father, their treachery demands the introduction – and application of God's penalty rule. Like in the game of English football, a penalty award serves a punitive measure against the errant team! God's penalty is His law and judgment, essentially aimed at correcting His errant but much loved ones.[5]

Additionally, the *law of reversal entry* of blessing *had* to come into effect. As harsh and sad as it may seem to the ears, the Creator God would issue a statement of curse on the serpent, the woman (Eve) and the man (Adam), in that specific order. The *law of reversal entry* of peace, for instance is war – and of course, for blessings, curses!

Therefore:

- *against the beguiling serpent,* God had pronounced these words of reversal entry:

"Because thou hast done this, thou art cursed above all cattle, and above every beast of the field; upon thy belly shalt thou go, and the dust shalt thou eat all the days of thy life ..."

Genesis 3:14

There is the word *"cursed"* glaringly seen in God's pronouncement against the serpent.

So what, indeed, is **the** *curse?*

The curse is **the** *decree uttered by the mouth of God which first nullifies, before proceeding in contrary motion, against the blessing!*

The curse institutionalizes the law of reversal entry. This is to say, if a thing was progressing – which is the proper, natural norm for its creation, if it becomes accursed; it *"super-matically"* begins its journey in retrogressing!

The curse therefore, is *the* empowerment to fail and not measure up to original, created purpose(s); *the* blessing on the other, is the exact opposite of *the* curse!

The curse – much like *the* blessing – to become effective, must be wished upon and uttered by *spirit-beings.*

The Creator Father *"God is a Spirit."* Since He is Spirit, He automatically is categorized as the primordial Spiritual Citizen #1, able to pronounce either *the blessing* or *the curse!* If anyone yields towards – and obeys His will, such becomes supernaturally, blessed. On the other hand, if someone contradicts any of His injunctions, they supernaturally become accursed under *the* Law.

Satan is also a spirit being. Though a spirit-being, he never created *a* thing. He also never promulgated *any* law! Thus, Satan, at no time ever had the jurisdictive power entirely reserved by *the* Creator. This is a huge limitation, which prohibits him from being able to utter either *the* blessing or *the* curse; only the Creator God reserves that special prerogative to operate, unrestrained in that realm – and *every* other!

This primary understanding surrounding the exclusive rights of the Creator Father, Friend, Judge and God ought to deal a huge relief to any whose livelihood is currently in turmoil; operating topsy-turvy, spiraling in and out of order and control! Superlatively, this translates that only God has *the* last say on *your* life – and surrounding circumstances. The devil does not; neither do his agents, wicked in-laws, parents/guardians, or a calculatedly mean boss! Only the Lord God Almighty, the Creator-Father-God-of-all, reserves the sole jurisdiction and prerogative to utter – or alter *the* curse and/or *the* blessing!

How, then, does the devil effect curses upon people?

The answer to that question is easy.

Since Satan does *not* reserve the prerogative to pronounce *the* curse, all he has to do to effect *a* curse upon a person or a group of people is re-enact the scenes of the original script played in the Garden of Eden, from person to person, people to people, nation to nation! He does this, primarily, by lying to, seducing and tempting them.

Satan's prime motive is to seduce, entice and tempt you to yield your will to act contrary to the Word of your Creator Father Friend! He'd always found his treachery ever so easy to achieve with the un-regenerated minds – that is, people who keep refusing Jesus Christ to become the Lord and Master of their lives – or indeed, any Christ-follower who refuses to renew their minds, daily! Otherwise, he has lost his upper biting teeth's ability to effect *any* curse whatsoever, upon you.[7]

Apart from God, then, who else can pronounce blessings or curses?

The onus of such a responsibility rests solely with the only remaining *spirit-beings*, called Mankind! Because *we* are essentially spirit-beings encased in bodies, possessing souls, *we* possess creative powers such as God, to invoke either *a* blessing or *a* curse. (Please note that it has been earlier mentioned that blessings or curses must *originate in the mind* – be *wished upon* and *released* – that is, spoken through the mouth, to become effective! Therefore, everyday words that *we* think about, conceive, speak or hear *are* potentially categorized as either *blessing* – if they are positive; or *curse* – if they are negative!

• *Against the serpent that beguiled Eve,* the Creator passed a new edict:

"Because thou hast done this, thou art cursed above all cattle, and above every beast of the field; upon thy belly shalt thou

go, and dust shalt thou eat all the days of thy life:

And I will put enmity between thee and the woman, and between thy seed and her seed; it shall bruise thy head, and thou shalt bruise his heel."

Genesis 3:14-15

- *Against Eve's tinkering with the tinderbox of rebellion, the Great Judge's anger sparked a proclamation of these retrogressive words:*

"I will greatly multiply thy sorrow and thy conception; in sorrow thou shalt bring forth children; and thy desire shall be to thy husband, and he shall rule over thee ... "

Genesis 3:16

- *Against Adam's treachery, the Creator pronounced these words:*

"Because thou hast hearkened unto the voice of thy wife, and hast eaten of the tree, of which I commanded thee, saying, Thou shalt not eat of it: cursed is the ground for thy sake; in sorrow shalt thou eat of it all the days of thy life;

Thorns also and thistles shall it bring forth to thee; and thou shalt eat of the herbs of the field; In the sweat of thy face shalt thou eat bread, till thou return unto the ground; for out of it wast thou taken: for dust thou art, and unto dust shalt thou return."

Genesis 3:17-19

That's a pretty heavy sentence against Adam; the severest pronouncement from the Creator's lips, a just reward for Adam's ir-reverence and disobedience! This is how God's justice system works; it smoothly works on an in-built, handsome, reward system! Like a coin on its reverse – or tail – side, the Creator's jurisdiction system bears the insignia of His law and judgment, death and hell! That is the true, reflective worth of His judicial prerogatives. However, there is also a corresponding, obverse side!

The obverse side of any currency/coin – popularly referred to as "the head" – bears the insignia of the authority-head! The *authority-head* of the Creator's judicial system portrays His unending loving-kindness, mercy, forgiveness and restoration!

Whatever your circumstance, situation or station in life's journey; whatever the cause of your brokenness, may you receive that inner strength to enable you begin learning to appreciate the gift of Father God's unending love, forgiveness, healing and restoration extended towards you. Amen!

Summary of Chapter 1

1.) Unforeseen and often un-anticipated adverse circumstances and disappointments in life's experiences *will* attempt to leave you bitter, frustrated, hopeless and broken, to say the very least. You must *not* allow yourself to be seduced onto the routes of negativity and pessimism!

2.) God can – and will – work through your life's various adverse seasons, *if* you let Him! His Word says:

"And we know that all things work together for good to them that love God, to them who are the called according to his purpose."[8]

3.) There was *the* Lamb that was slain, whose fleece covered Adam and Eve's joint nakedness; *the* perfect sacrifice just for you, your family or home. The sacrifice of this "Lamb of God" generated His shed blood that wipes clean the sins of generations unborn. This is God's perfect, all-time-best Gift; just for *y-o-u!*

Mending a Broken Heart

With the help of a Bible concordance or dictionary, find instance(s) where phrases such as: *"it grieved God's heart"*, *"it repented God"* – and words such as *"rejection"*, *"rejected"*, *"sin"*, *"forgiveness"*, *"grace"* and *"redemption"* occur. Study them – and compile notes. Take time to do a thorough, extensive research.

Excellent additional book resources that would help you understand the Father's love and mend a broken heart are:

1.) Led to Believe by Billy Graham; GuidepostsBooks, 2007.

2.) GOD'S Remedy for Rejection by the late author, Derek Prince; Whitaker House, 1993.

The message in 'The Gift of Restoration' burned within my very core as I wrote specifically for you who eternally yearn for a longing to be accepted without bias, prejudice or blame, accepted for who you are, just as you are!

"Mercy and truth have met together; righteousness and peace have kissed each other ...

Yes, the Lord will give what is good, and our land will yield her increase."

The Psalmist

Chapter 2

The Gift of Restoration

"For I will restore health unto thee, and I will heal thee of thy wounds, saith the LORD; because they called thee an outcast ..."

Jeremiah 30:17

We've either been brought up that way or societal expectations have tutored us well; yet this is the harsh reality: encounter *anything* that has been scratched, cracked, broken or damaged – and we drop or dump it in a jiffy! Learning how or why it bears its less-than-perfect distinguishing scar is of primary non-importance.

I'd gone shopping with my teenaged daughter, Gabriella, the other day at her favorite store – and from the very corner of my eye had witnessed her pick a carton of eggs without first checking the contents – *as she'd been taught to do!*

"Oh-la-la-aa-a," I muttered, as I instinctively reached out to flip open the plastic egg carton's encasement in her hands. Confirming my worst expectation, there it was, smiling at us both: a dented, widely cracked shell! With

wide-opened, bulging pair of lovely eyes as mine, I'd motioned her: *"D-U-M-P the carton – and pick another!"*

Now, while my instinctive reaction may have been *earthly* economically sound; it certainly was not *heavenly* economically viable to the loving heavenly Father, the "Father of spirits."[1]

When life has you *scratched, cracked, broken and damaged* – guess people's instinctual reaction? They would dump – and wash their hands off you with the quickest alacrity! They possibly would *not* want anything to do with you. (Some would actually throw you into the bin, condemned to rot away on a destined waste-yard!)

One major mistake the *unregenerate* man makes is his failure to realize that *no human* is an economical good. Plainly put, no human is *just* human! I know that rocks your foundation to its roots; but the truth is: *humans* are essentially spirit-beings! We'd better be *very* conscientious how we treat other 'spirit-beings' – that we do *not* incur unvoiced wrath!

- *Have you ever been "scratched", "cracked", "abused", "broken" or "damaged"?*

- *Do you know any who has been forsaken and neglected, 'dumped' in the bin like a soiled Huggies pamper?*

- *Do you personally, feel rejected?*

I have *Goodnews* for you!

Humanity too was damaged in the peaceful Garden of Eden

by a very pungent pollutant called sin. Anything *sin* came in contact with automatically reverted towards corruption and death.[2] Needless to say, a toss of God's coin of justice demanded that Man be set for the scrap-yard of an everlasting corruption in the abyss of an eternal hell. However, His Father-heart elected the coin's obverse; the options of restoration and redemption of *His* creation and ace creature, mankind! This Father-God possesses an abundance of mercy and compassion in the face of His judgment's demands!

God's Restoration – the Blessing

If you'd ever been involved in an accident and had needed your vehicle restored, the word *'restoration'* would bear you the semblances of deep, touching emotions!

When I'd been involved in a car accident, *December '06*, that had totally written off my '*L reg.*' 1994 Toyota Lucida van, I'd been offered the choices to sell for scrap, spares – or engage in restorative chasis-rendering. Because of my love for vintage, I'd opted for the latter! Soon, I had been referred to a *Bodyworks* guy who had done a most perfect restorative job. Today, you could never ever tell it was the same old *go-getter!*

In a more pronounced way, if *only* you would allow Father God to carry out extensive reconstructive surgeries within your 'heart', I most honestly would assure you that people would argue between themselves if it ever was the same *you* who had undergone His surgery![3] This is because in mercy and grace, the Creator Father-God longs to *"restore to you the years that the locust hath eaten, the cankerworm, and the caterpillar, and the palmerworm, my great*

29

army which I sent among you."[4]

Yes, His essence as the Judge and Arbiter of *the law* calls for a swift penalty of a *"great army"* to set in and plunder us, in response to our rebellion. Believably, in His mercy however, *Daddy* longs to bless, heal and restore health unto His children's navels and marrow to their bones.[5] Also, the hands of this merciful heavenly Father longs to re-mold *our* brokenness, as does the hands of a crafty Potter.[6]

Remember, *the curse,* brought rejection; *the blessing,* acceptance in the beloved![7] *The curse* the great 'falling apart'; *the blessing,* redemption and restoration of the fallen, trodden upon and broken! Pulverize it as you may, *the* blessing is Father God's restoration masterpiece; *His* greatest gift of all!

Notice with me a few things *the* blessing entails:

- *The blessing is the divine empowerment to operate stress-free, successfully – and successively on the arena called life.*

- *The blessing supernaturally performs "the law of reversal entry" on the curse.*

- *The blessing divinely enables to prosper, succeed, be fruitful and multiply instead of failure in a withering, shrinking global economy.*

- *The blessing earns you acceptance instead of rejection!*

- *The blessing is in effect, when instead of a deserved verdict of "Guilty", the defendant's attentive ears – hears the Judge return a verdict of "Not guilty!"*

- *The blessing "that maketh rich and addeth no sorrows" is the greatest Gift of all, an erring humanity can ever receive from a gracious Father-Creator!*

The Father's Re-assurance

No matter the depth of your depravity and ills, regardless of the damage earned you by hurts, betrayals and brokenness suffered; like Ephraim of old, God's paternal heart longs to accept, forgive and restore you.

Hear the cockles of His heart, ask:

> *"Is Ephraim My dear son? Is he a darling child and beloved? For as often as I speak against him, I do [earnestly] remember him still. Therefore My affection is stirred and My heart yearns for him; I will surely have mercy, pity, and loving-kindness for him, says the Lord."*
>
> Jeremiah 31:20; Amplified Version

Now, in the place of *Ephraim,* substitute your name into that verse of scripture, above – and personalize the re-assurance of your Father's love for *you.*

On another page written by Isaiah the prophet, we read:

> *"Behold, it was for my peace that I had intense bitterness; but You have loved my life from the pit of corruption and nothingness, for You have cast all my sins behind Your back."*
>
> Isaiah 38:17

Not only will you find Father God's unconditional love

31

and pardon, readily; you will receive in addition, His re-empowerment and restoration in full measure!

In the tranquility of the Garden of Eden after pronouncing the *First Judgment* upon the serpent and the first couple, God's Father-heart demonstrated *this* unique essence of His unconditional love, pardon and "covering" by miraculously providing them, fleece from *the* Lamb! That 'covering lamb' was *the Lamb of God that was slain.*[8] This, in a nutshell, is the mystery of restoration of mankind to God. That Lamb, fleeced for the covering of Adam and Eve's nakedness was *symbolic* of Christ Jesus, slain for us at the Cross of Calvary.

Receive a Wholesome Restoration

When my book *"Destroying the Power of Delay: Possessing Your Canaan"* was released Fall 2011, *PULSE Publishing House* took an initiative to offer *freely* – inclusive of packaging and mailing – to anyone who would request their copy within the time frame of thirty days of the month of December. The response was so phenomenal; we *had* to wisely restrict ourselves to *"just a copy per day per household!"*

You would presume that everyone appreciated our sincerest gestures to publish and spread the liberating Gospel of the Lord! Quite to the contrary. Some skeptics wrote in from our backyard, to question both the genuineness and the motive behind our offer. Others, some, wrote in disbelief as to *"Why should we succumb to your temptation-offer of a useless free gift?"*

I was very disheartened, to say the least!

Soon, God would prove the skeptics wrong: the book continues to bless the countless lives that have encountered the messages within its covers in various countries of the world up until this very day. Here's the connecting vital truth: to the English mentality, the idea of offering no-payment for a quality good was totally alien; it would be welcomed with thorough skepticism.

To many others, still, receiving a gift was absolutely alien to their thought-processes – because they probably never gave one beyond Christmas. This is our "tradition".

Similarly, whenever we wear the sunshades of *our* christian traditions, these unrestrainedly act as "filters", filtering in dispersion, the bright rays of love and acceptance, emanating from the Father of lights!

The Father heart of God offers us *"good and perfect gifts."* His most precious Gift is in the person of *the Lamb of God*, Jesus Christ!

The Father heart of this Creator-Restorer expects *you* to receive *His* Gift of love into *your* heart by faith. This *Gift* then becomes *yours* for keeps – *the* indescribable and unspeakable everlasting love of the Father!

> *"See what [an incredible] quality of love the Father has given (shown, bestowed on) us, that we should [be permitted to] be named and called and counted the children of God! And so we are!"*
>
> 1 John 3:1; Amplified Version.

33

Summary of Chapter 2

I will summarize the just concluded chapter with words from the Father heart of God through one of His prophets, Isaiah:

1.) Damaged people could be willful; but because the Father heart of God sees their weaknesses and ways, He will heal them.

2.) The broken-hearted may have become blind due to their brokenness, yet the Father Creator says He will lead them.

3.) People who have suffered various injustices and abuse would have suffered heavy losses and become heavily bruised in the process. But thus says the Lord: *"I will recompense and restore comforts unto them"*; and finally,

4.) People who have become "cracked" may not have many to mourn with them, but the few faithful who – understand their plight and – mourn with them *"shall be refreshed"*.

Isaiah 57:18-19

"Blessed are they who mourn, for they shall be comforted."
Master Jesus

Do you receive these words?

A Wholesome Restoration

An excellent additional book resource that could be helpful in your restoration is:

Peace with God by Rev. Dr. Billy Graham, first published in 1953 by *Thomas Nelson Publishers U.S.A.* Revised edition published in 1984 by *World Wide Publications, U.S.A.*

'The Gift of a True Friendship' is a brief reference tool for all persons who aspire to spruce up their friendships; especially those contemplating finding, pursuing, entering into – and abiding in a loving relationship.

"A man that hath friends must shew himself friendly ..."
King Solomon;
the world's wisest man.

Chapter 3

The Gift of a True Friendship

"A friend loveth at all times, and a brother is born for adversity."

Proverbs 17:17

A beautiful, young lady – whom we shall call Lovett, not her real name, and a dashing young man – George, not his real name – both Campus students, met – and from the beginning, hit "an item." Soon they promised each other loyalty and true friendship that soon led to true love! They bid time just to complete their formal education. Upon completion, they became engaged. Barely half a year later, they were married.

It wasn't a surprise to both parents from either side; they had anticipated and "geared up" for their children's big day, saving hard, for it. All had gone well.

During their romantic honeymoon, which had lasted a week on a remote island in the Caribbean, the newlyweds had renewed their loyalty incessantly! *Almost hourly!* Those were the "wee hours" of a long-haul romance.

The reality of moving into their new *pad* – and transitioning into a proper married life schedule soon dawned upon them as their departure date drew ever closer. Looking rather agitated, George, then, posed this question to his wife:

"Would you be willing to perform a request for me when I die?"

Surprised at the unexpected awkward question, the confused young bride retorted: *"You are not going to die now; we are in our bloom-days! What in the world are you talking about?"* She showed her displeasure at the motion of current of the discussion; she wasn't in the mood for *his* antics, that lazy Saturday afternoon!

Some people, naturally, are 'worriers'. It never dawned on Lovett that she had – for the rest of her life – bagged herself a 'worrier' for a hubby! Nevertheless, a few more weeks, the same scenario replayed itself – this time, with a distinctive difference: Lovett found herself concurring to George's request that they visit their attorney. The attorney, acting under George's instructions would draft George's will, in case the inevitable occurred sooner than expected!

That had sounded very reasonable! However, months went by, closely followed by years – and nothing drastic, had occurred! Instead, two adorable children – a boy and a girl – had completed their family setting.

Before long, those children had graduated from elementary into high school, then College – and finally, the University. George, too, had climbed the corporate ladder after many years of hard work. Lovett had remained a dutiful wife, a trusted confidant, an eagled-eyed house-manager and a godly mother.

What more could they have asked for?

Both lovebirds, now well into their 70's, had become grandparents with some conspicuous strands of grey hairs. Grandpa George had had more to his hairline, though; he had the likeness of a glowing miter at his crown! He had now retired. Grandama Lovett, on the other hand hadn't retired: her job specification had actually increased with the onslaught of five healthy grand-children, successively, whom they baby-sat from time to time!

Living, for both couple, had been a lifetime of togetherness, accomplishments and huge investments. Moreover, their love life had grown beyond imaginable depths.

Soon again, the ageing, impetuous George had requested that the couple visit their attorney. He'd somehow convinced Lovett, he'd love to incorporate – an amendment and a clause into his will. "Fine", she had agreed!

These were the exact new wordings of an extract of George's emerging will:

"That in the eventuality of my demise, my life-savings be divided into four-quarters: two-quarters of which are to be given to my beloved wife and sweetheart, herewith named, Lovett ____; a quarter shared equally between our grandchildren – and the last quarter due to me.

My wife, named above shall enclose my apportioned sum in an envelope, place in my right hand and bury with me for my sustenance in after-life!"

Those instructions seemed understandable to wife!

The inevitable finally occurred, five years later – and Lovett had been grief-stricken!

At the graveside committal service, a close family friend who was privy to the couples' integrity and unquestionable dedication to and love for each other winked at the distressed, immaculately dressed widow in black – and whispered in a hush-voice: *"I sure bet I could fault your loyalty to George on one premise. Could you indeed have buried with him, his apportionment?"*

The graceful widow forced a rueful smile, before gently nodding! *"Yes, I did indeed honor George's wishes;"* she re-assured. *"I wrote him a check for the equivalent amount of his apportionment, placed it in a sealed envelope and forced it in-between his fingers before lowering the casket's lid!"*

Major Ingredients of a True Friendship

"A man that hath friends must show himself friendly: and there is a friend that sticketh closer than a brother."

Proverbs 18:24

In these days of friendship farce, what are the major characteristic ingredients that should be akin to a true friendship?

Emphatically, I will limit myself to mentioning just some

of those *basic* ingredients that will firmly set the roots of your potted, budding seedling of friendship in an enriched soil. Here they are:

i.) Early acknowledgement of the source of your friendship:

Foremost on my list of factors that must be firmly set in place before you commence friendship, is an early requirement of an *"acknowledgement!"* An acknowledgement that leads to a realization that *either* the Creator-Father *or* His stark opponent, the Destroyer-Satan orchestrated *this* friendly prospect.

In other words, you must *not* take for granted *your* crossing of tracks with this new friendship. You, determine early, *who* it was in the spiritual realm that initiated it. Remember, no two pathways ever did cross just for a mere *happenstance*.

Once you have firmly established the *origin* of your new friendship, you must now set your mind upon discovering what *particular work* God is doing, arranging your pathways to meet, should you have acknowledged the heavenly Father as the Facilitator! Answers to such questions, as *"Are they a friend for a reason, a season or a lifetime?"* must be sought intimately, in prayer.

Additionally, ask the Lord questions such as:

- *"What am I supposed to accomplish in their life?"*

- *"Are they just an acquaintance or a keeper?"*

Never approach *any* friendship with either an obvious or a hidden mindset of what *they* could primarily do for you; but rather, with a harnessed mindset of what *you* could accomplish through God, *for* them! Here's the key: the prime motives of *"empowerment"* and *"giving the advantage"* over to a friend are very crucial to a healthy start off *any* friendship blocks! Purpose, at all costs, to be *the* healthy friend!

ii.) Need for knowledge:

As time progresses, you will also request information from your new friend, practically by communication. You will likely eventually communicate face to face. If you live in further proximity away from each other, you may communicate by *Skype* and video-phone conversation, e-mail – or other suitable mediums, as time and opportunity avail you. Open-ended communication will help ascertain the level of depth to which you both should "pitch" your friendship!

Other necessary ingredients that will encourage your friendship to bud include:

iii.) Trust,
iv.) Integrity,
v.) Truthfulness, and;
vi.) Loyalty to common causes and interests.

Friendships deepen roots when these variables are incorporated:

vii.) Timely openness,
viii.) Mutual sincerity, respect and admiration – never forgetting the impact,
ix.) The ability and willingness to inject fun and

laughter into your lives; laughing together with and at each other!

If *your* heart possesses these fundamental *basics*, you will *not* fail to naturally draw and magnetize hearts.

Growing Gracefully into the Different Seasons of Friendship

Friendship, like other endeavors of life, has its due seasons!

As your friendship settles and tangles roots with the soil of the other person's heart, you would soon realize that it requires more than just *'the basics'* of the spring season of discovering each other, to blossom and bear fruits. Grow, therefore, deepening roots through the spring into the summer season of friendship, keeping the richness, health and vitality of your friendship soils with such *additives* as:

- *Vulnerability,*

- *Transparency,*

- *Knowledge, wisdom, and understanding,*

- *Tact, and;*

- *Selflessness.*

In the *Fall or Wintry season* of your friendships, keep handy such *re-growth additives* as:

- *Forgiveness,*

- *Sensitivity to each other's needs or lack,*

- *Exchange of gifts, re-defining boundaries – and keeping within such boundaries;*

- *Ability to lovingly confront wrongs with the aim of restoration, and;*

- *A wholesome demonstration of a genuine sense of dedication.*

These will prepare both hearts in readiness to usher in *spring*, a season of bloom, to your potted friend-seedlings!

Let's briefly discuss each of these "additives"!

1. Vulnerability originating from genuine and godly openness:

When someone has a *secret agenda* or a hidden, impure motive for desiring friendship, the first tool they would deploy is "holding out!" Undue restrain of self from being discovered and/or "holding out" useful pieces of information that would potentially help the other party determine whether or not they would want to further desire friendship becomes a deliberate ploy at self-preservation!

Some other times, people who have suffered rejection, emotional or physical wounds due to abuse usually have a huge task *opening up* to new friendship(s) that could potentially bring them blessings. They may *not* be able to afford being vulnerable. Vulnerability is that quintessential ingredient necessary for a true and effective bonding in *all* friendships! Yet, it is *the* super glue that most friendships lack!

Now, if your friend lacks either the ability or willingness

to become vulnerable with you, put into practice, these four suggestions:

First, be mindful of an appropriate timing to raise an inquiry:
Search the depths of *your* heart if indeed, it was the right timing for you to know the reason behind their *"holding out."*

Second, ensure your emotional preparedness and wholeness:
Ensure that you are emotionally whole and sound – and wouldn't react with a flinch, a surprised look, a hurt or a rejection to their story should they judge it O.K. to *open up* to you. Make sure you do *not* laugh at them either! Most times when the issue of non-vulnerability had evolved, the "vulnerable" first shares a slight "introduction", sits back and watches your reactions, using them as gauges to ascertain your readiness/un-readiness for the *news proper* they've got for your ears, *only!*

While you prompt your entire being in readiness to listen and "learn", again, please do *not* laugh at them, neither wear a 'smiley' face! Get a firm hold of your posture that you do *not* appear as 'uptight' either, as to convey an attitude of irreverence or the looks of overt-seriousness that would make you appear false and imitative!

Third, do not resort to pressure-tactics:
Never demand, neither pressurize anyone to become "vulnerable" with you. Rather, nurture them with plenty of trust and re-assurances that have originated from a true, sincere, friendly heart.

I have always re-assured new acquaintances: *"I am a genuine minister of God and wouldn't take advantage of your weakness, nor let you take advantage of me!"* You may want to declare likewise sincerity to your new friend! Beware, such honesty and sincerity will certainly freak some people out!

Fourth, engage patience and calmness:
Patience and calmness are virtues that come with soul-discipline. No human was born with an automatic propensity to be patient. Like all virtues, you *have* to learn to cultivate it. When you've demonstrated virtues that you intrinsically possess, it wouldn't be difficult to win hearts!

2. Transparency and honesty which should not be employed as 'control mechanisms':

Some people, within minutes of your first meeting have narrated *all* their victories, sorrows and woes; you hardly could understand why they seemed to lack an ounce of discretion! The reason for their display of foolhardiness is not far-fetched: most often times, people who lack discretion, setting a guard over their hearts are either psychologically or pathologically impaired. Except again, they are relationship control freaks! Theirs is an unhealthy transparency; the style of most friendship-fraudsters!

Healthy minds on the other hand, steer a mile and a post clear of manipulation. They know just when to *open up* or *close up!* They are honest to a fault – without any inhibiting fears of recrimination or remonstration.

3. Knowledge, wisdom, tact and understanding:

With wisdom, ask questions – in order to gain insight into your friend's personality. Do *not* assume an answer. If your friend is shy, thus not asking questions, that might be a signal to you that *they* would prefer the option of a provision of leading questions.

Like a leash, affording a new pet-keeper/owner the rare privilege of dictating safe or convenient boundaries within which that pet may explore, leading questions afford you the rare privilege of setting the pace or dictating the parameters of discovery you are willing to avail your new, shy friend!

Leading questions are primarily designed to draw out a person's or people's intents. They gently goad towards an inclination. There is absolutely no wrong done when you gently prod an acquaintance with a question such as: *"I am just wondering if you wouldn't wear a wristwatch because of its corrosive impact on you or because you have an allergy against wearing any band around your wrist?"* You then pause, using their response as an efficient gauge to measure their responsiveness! If after throwing *your* ice-breaker, they still wouldn't budge, it could be that they are the *analytic-minded personality*.

Analytical-minded folk process and internalize data, mostly! This in no way suggests that they are *not* interested in developing friendship or vulnerability with you.

On the other hand, if your friend keeps re-butting your efforts and attempts at encouraging them to *'open up'* over time, it could mean that they do not desire friendship with you! Only *you* would decide whether to *stay moored* or *move on!* Beware of demanding, draining, "hang-over", burdensome friends!

Some people exist at the station of loneliness or boredom. Some currently, may be working through a difficult situation in their lives – having only requested for *just* companion-friendship. You, on the other hand are searching for a potential mate! Agreeably, so glaring it is, that your attempt to quicken the pace of your friendship status onto that of falling in love/lovers will, in all likelihood, lead to your eventual, complete fall-out, both. *Why?* This is because your individual needs – or what I call *friendship-specs* exist diametrically opposite each other's! Charles C. Colson's affirmation cannot be truer: friendships may end in love; not *vice versa!*

Other times, someone may secretly desire a deeper friendship with you but are genuinely too broken to "let go" of themself. If this were the case, your being an honorable, appreciable gift, gifted such a person would be your willing intent to mend their brokenness – and nurture them to health again. Nothing short of this would be the Creator-Father's expectation of you! Your efforts accepting, loving and showing them love would be symbolic of that exquisite, *agape* kind of love that He first bequeathed on us! Your dealing them the *"agape dosage"* certainly will require a fair deal of patience, knowledge and understanding of their shortcomings – even as the Heavenly Father possesses of His tainted ace-creation: humanity!

Additional to your possessing the heavenly Father-kind of love, be full of tact. A guy would be *really* dumb to *not* know that he should never refer directly or indirectly to his girl/lady friend's size or weight, either in conversation, by a sideway corner-of-the-eye look, gesticulations or instincts. Either accept what endowments nature has bequeathed her with or quietly pass her by! Sincere compliments, however, would win anyone's heart – any day!

Equally strangely naive it would be for a lady to play down as un-important, the nagging issue of her male friend's lack of a means to support his livelihood, because she has fallen head over heels in love with him! She could be a hardworking, successful – probably executive-type – female who, nevertheless, has set herself up for potential abuse of various sorts in the name of love! Or she could be a '*time-runner*'; someone who lacks discretion and insight – a lady smitten by a selfish need to get "hooked up", shack with or get married, at all cost! Probably she was a billionaire's heiress on a remote island! Even at that, a lady's seemingly flippant attitude towards a *scum-bug* is an obvious sign of either plain stark stupidity or an undiagnosed insanity! Such ladies later realize that the *in-love* feeling never in history, ever pacified an angry *Mr. Bills* who stands aggressively, knocking lovers' entrance doors, each calendar month-end!

A *true* woman *in love* acknowledges that a *true* man has severe debilitating mental tortures if he hasn't a decent means to support they whom he *truly* loves!

4. Selflessness:

If your friendship is gravitating towards selfishness, you need to roll up your sleeves and realize there's some apportioned homework awaiting *your* tackling! Sometimes, selfishness presents itself so subtly that it rarely is easy to recognize. For instance, when a friend begins to place on the other, demands and orders – as done at takeaway restaurants – instead of polite requests, it would be time for *you* to lovingly confront him/her.

5. Forgiveness:

A friendship or an alliance untested by offences and

hurts, simply, *may not* withstand the test of time. Offences surely must come, the antidote; ready forgiveness!

Forgiving an offender is entirely dependent on the state of the heart of the forgiver. Forgiveness cannot be hushed up nor demanded. There is however, a liberating feeling you attain when you freely forgive *your* offender. Forgive today – and more often, therefore!

6. Sensitivity to each other's needs or lack:
There are certain appropriate gestures that would be deemed inappropriate if practiced at wrong times. Let me give you a practical illustration. If your friend is bereaved, courtesy demands that you be of a few words – or none at all!

Be sensitive enough to recognize that they are grieving and as such would require *some* space and time to do so, appropriately! Your presence though, would be most valued and appreciated above all else!

Other than your meaningful presence, you could hug and hold them tight, for a few, quick seconds, depending on how close your bond with them is! Otherwise, you may just lightly lay your hand upon their shoulder, as to re-affirm to them: *"All will be well!"* You could also place their hand(s) in yours, and squeeze lightly.

Present them a bouquet of flowers you know they would cherish – accompanied by an appropriate card. Ensure you have carefully chosen *that* card. Normally, a card with a plain inside upon which you could personally address them, in carefully chosen words of condolence would be most appropriate. Nothing else could be as golden!

Actions speak louder than words at moments of bereavement; so let your words be few!

Conversely, the gift of a true friendship begins in service. Do *not* wait for your friend to verbalize their need of crucial help in excruciating moments – before you have offered two helpful hands and a couple of sensitive feet. Be sensitive to the *"still, small voice"* within!

7. Timeliness of purpose and exchange of gifts that convey your heart's message:

'Doing favors' for friends and gift-exchanges between mates are positive signs of budding growth in the friendship process. Ensure sincerity of motives, though, when you exchange gifts with the people you claim to befriend or love.

Do *not* offer them second-to-best, next-to-nothing, less-than-perfect gifts.

If you intend to offer their children, for instance, clothes that your children have outgrown, ensure first, that you have asked the parent(s)/guardian(s) of your intended benefactors. Some parents may be so easily offended even by the very best of intents.

If you are the only "giver" or "pursuer" in *your* friendship, for instance, this ought to be a tell-tale sign *yours* is already a stale, lame-duck. It would do you no good trying to flog it. Try searching for a cute little robin that chirps!

Does a gift have to be costly in order to become acceptable?

No!

A collection of ordinary, ripe, wild, white daisy flowers handpicked on a field on your way home – accompanied by a cute note on a card that says: *"Y-O-U Alone, My Purity; My Love!"* could indicate to your friend or loved-one that you had *him/her* on your mind all day! That simple flower and note may communicate to a wife her appreciable "worth" far more than the expensive, *Marks & Spencer* sexy thong and bra/lingerie outfit you're dying to order! If a wife were to present her hubby with that kind of a note, oh my; she certainly will succeed sending his head into a spin, faster than her washing machine or tumble dryer!

Appreciably too is a surprise, romantic holiday at a romantic spot, *just* for both of you. That may just happen to be the right tonic needful to rev up your friendship and relationship – and add stamina to your love lives!

8. Define boundaries early in your friendship/relationship:

Effective healthy boundaries are workable, understandable guidelines between friends regarding the *do's* and *don't's*, *acceptable* and *unacceptable* terms of their friendship/relationship.

Delineate and define, early enough, the boundaries of your friendship. Be mindful to respect – and *not* transgress such boundaries. Preferably, dwell within an appreciable margin *away from* your delineation. Any friend who cannot be bothered about boundary setting from the on-start of a friendship/relationship should have been revealed as potentially, a *nifty-shifty* personality!

How do I know? I know because "boundaries" and "restraints" are two English words, the generality of people hate with a passion!

Always ensure that you and your friend/significant other have a perfect understanding of healthy expectations of each other. State and re-iterate from time to time, the purpose(s) of your friendship/relationship to both be relevant and current, still "on the same page."

9. The ability to lovingly confront without harboring feelings of hatred or rejection from either party:

True friendship grants to the other full, unreserved rights to *"speak life"* into each other's life! This is one great method of keeping balance. True friends mirror each other's unperceived image, in turns. Iron must authoritatively continue to sharpen iron; not bronze, wood or glass. When either you or your friend have become too scared to speak life into each other's lives, citing fear in a statement as: *"I was just too scared as not to hurt your feelings"*; ah, alas, something has gone drastically wrong! You both have become too 'glassy' – and are sliding into an error of insincerity, dishonesty and possibly, heresy!

When they have begun to avoid you, you must, in the spirit of wisdom seek them out with the spirit of understanding undergirding their error(s), like the Father heart of God had sought out Adam and Eve, in the garden of Eden!

True friendship *"speaks the truth in love."*

True friendship operates within the parameters of that heavenly wisdom easily placated; that is, yielding to reason. This heavenly wisdom neither nurses hurts nor rehearses wrongs done it.

Wisdom from above operates within the parameters of true love that forgives, with the aim to restore and nurture to wholeness.

True friendship does *not* esteem itself higher, above constructive criticisms. Even the Father-heart of God calls us friends; He did *not* place Himself above Moses' erstwhile counsel in the wilderness!

True friendship is reflective!

If you have to correct a friend, first and foremost:

i.) Ensure that you ask God to give you a meek heart.

ii.) Re-assure them you always have their best interests at heart.

iii.) Do not recriminate or remonstrate with them, their error(s):
Remember you are *not* their Judge, you are their friend! Try *not* to give them a lesson in morals and ethics; neither hurl the Holy Scriptures at them: it's like pouring icy water on a head on a wintry night.

Remember to be loyal to your friend – and esteem them – even in their faults.

iv.) Be full of tact:
It is lesser than virtuous to re-quote an errant friend's

statements to them – or indeed another! Be civil and courteous, always. Sentences beginning with *"Your exact words were _____"* would end up disastrous! You very well know that even you detest being re-quoted to your face, when you've been in the wrong!

Again, remember you're not in a court of jurisdiction, so be gentle, kind – yet full of truth and grace!

v.) Offer intercessory prayers to the Father "God of all flesh" for their needs:
Be kind enough to lift them up in your daily intercessory prayers, too. Prophet Samuel continued to pray for the disdained King Saul until his death!

vi.) Be prepared to restore them if God gives them a repentant heart:
In other words, don't shut the door firmly in their face; leave at least the spy-hole, unblocked! Never say *"Never", if* the Lord hasn't decreed it!

10. Lastly, recognize and demonstrate genuine focused dedication at your primary calling:
If as earlier advised, you recognized your friendship/ relationship as *keepers*; never let go, come what may! Some people are *not* focused enough to deepen roots in friendship/relationship; no sooner had they encountered a turbulence in their flight-path had they jettisoned the friend Heaven assigned them, in search of a new one, *flesh* intimated them with.

Jettisoning *keeper-friendship* flight-paths hasn't been made any easier in particular, than when people have refused to recognize and adhere to their primary places of divine assignments. Do *not* blame Facebook, Twitter and the advent of the social media for your ill-moral, abandoning of your duty-post thus forfeiting the reward-points that only the discipline of dedicated focus brings.

A gentleman by the name, Stephanas and his household had discovered their primary positions of assignments – and had focused on them. They understood what I am sharing with you! Although young converts to the way of Christ, the Stephanas's had *"addicted themselves"* in total devotedness and dedication to the service of God's people. No wonder, St. Paul the aged urged his Corinthian readers to *"pay all deference to such leaders and to enlist under them and be subject to them"* (1 Corinthians 16:15-16; *Amplified Version*).

This story about the Stephanas's only reinforces the fact that there are *regrets*, the early recognition of your place of primary assignment will spare you – and *dividends* only the force of focus will ultimately yield!

These *additives* will encourage the 'deepening of roots' of your newfound enterprise, friend or relationship. Apply them today – and witness the green fresh foliage of your friendship offshoot new blooms!

Lessons to Help Enhance Your Friendship

I am not a person of large "inner-circle" friends. However, the few special relationships – in particular, the enriching individual friendships – with each of *my quivers* and very close associates have taught me invaluable lessons that

I know will help enhance you and your friendships/ relationships. Be warned, these lessons will remain with you, for a lifetime!

Lesson #1 ~ If you are in need, never lay a demand; rather, present a request:

Placing a demand on people depicts your personality as bossy, disrespectful and extremely irritable.

By Father God's special anointing upon me, I have single-handedly raised my five children since *2005* through a separation that degenerated into a bitter divorce. The divorce concurrently escorted me hand-in-hand into the family courtroom in a four-year judicial stint that centered upon the children's residency/custody. Sometimes, on a day when I had been well spent, laundered and dried, I would most certainly have come across as either touchy, gruffly or bossy! On such days, I had instinctively placed *demands* on those closest to me, without even realizing it.

One particular, bitterly cold wintry evening, when I had thought it all done for the day; suddenly, I'd received an *SOS* call. This had emanated from one of the families in the church. My urgent attention had been summoned to an emergency. The father had been away at work that evening but their beautiful teenaged daughter's hormones had risen to a new high; she had walked out of the family home – into the dark cold streets and frozen, thin air!

Instinctively, I had asked my children who had all been dressed up for bed, to change into *casuals* – not forgetting their coats, gloves, hats and scarves. We had *had* to go out!

I had rushed downstairs and looked for the bunch that contained the car keys. In such a hasty moment, I'd never thought it harmful to ask *Prissy* –then six, my precious little girl who naturally loves to be dutiful, to *"Go back upstairs and get the bunch of keys from atop the cabinet in my room!"*

That sounds like a simple, comprehensible request, doesn't it?

But wait!

That same night I *had* been taught an unforgettable lesson! It is same lesson I now share with you. The tired, sleepy-eyed, little toddler cocked her head at an angle, rolled her eyes at me and demanded: *"You too need to learn to add the magic word, Dad; or I wouldn't budge."*

"Oh, I am absolutely sorry, my darling; you know that I've always been a polite daddy", I voiced, as I fumbled around for an apologetic embrace!

The forgotten word for which *my* Prissy had reprimanded me was *'please'*. That's my children's "magic word" – that word "magic" being loosely used since we never believed in nor practiced magic!

The Joseph clan had been brought up to be polite little gems; however, one nimble hearted diamond had caught the trainer's lips off-guard in a moment that had turned out be his moment of *one* rude-awakening! Prissy had rightly taught me that *placing a demand begets a demand!*

Instead of being demand-full, be polite!

Adding *'please'* either as a prefix *before* or as a suffix *after* a request simply shows excellent manners. Construct your requests to fellow beings – and even pets – regardless of ages, color or creed, adding *'please.'*

"Could I have _____ please?" Or *"Please can you help get _____?"*

"Please" is a powerful word that persuades against the stoniest of hearts. Politeness is the key used by persons of authority to unlock and turn their subordinates' hearts towards attaining the corporate vision or goal. My children call it the "magic word". Adults call it *courtesy.*

Demand begets demand; respect engenders the same.

Never forget to be courteous and respectful in your friendships. And please, never place a demand in your relationships. Be humble, yet meek. Meekness has been defined as *'Strength, broken, and under control!'*

Lesson #2 ~ Be lavish and extravagant in your approbations and praise:

Almost three decades ago as a university undergraduate, I'd stumbled upon the late American author, Dale Carnegie's most influencing book: *"How To Win Friends And Influence People."* I must admit, each lesson on those two-hundred-and-ninety-one pages – one of which bears the #2 sub-title – had stuck with me ever since: "BE EXTRAVAGANT IN PRAISE."

Always find that extra, praiseworthy commendable and appreciable quality in your spouse, lover, friend, child(ren), family, subordinates or employees and acquaintances –

and rightfully commend/praise them!

I am *not* talking about flattery; for it is a major ill under the category of subtlety and deceit. Rather, I am advocating for the free-flow of praise, praise, praise – and more praise! Show me *any* human who cringes in the sight of an honest praise; you probably won't find any! The truth is that we *all* love praises; our littlest achievements, recognized. Indeed, we strike a contrast with our heavenly Creator-Father; He also loves praises. Every human owes that "want-of-praise" character trait to Him.

Always recognize, identify and praise the feeblest of efforts your friend, spouse, child, or employee has endeared toward you.

When the artists in our home drew and presented dad a "gift of art", a special recognition was given! I still possess up until this day, Paul's, Prissy's and Gabby's drawings when they were three or four years old. Occasionally, many years later when I had wanted to be *extra-ordinary*, I had ascended into the loft and descended with short tons of children's wild sketches, for us all to see, laugh – and reminisce about all day, on a lazy Saturday afternoon!

What point am I trying to reinforce?

Do *not* take people's worth for granted. Do not keep people's potentials, stifled! Acknowledge, recognize and verbalize your praise of them!

I often reward my children with a smothering, 'spiky' peck on their smooth cheeks. *Does Dad kiss the boys also?*

Oh yeah; for sure! How they love it! No wonder, they unanimously found me, overnight, a befitting nickname: *'Spiky!'* Some of you parents can't even conceive of the idea of *your* children 'nick-naming' you; in all honesty, you don't know what gifted opportunities for bonding you're missing out upon. You'd need to have a re-think!

Recently as I added another year, my *Dannyboy* – who could be very fluent in my exact type of sarcasm and dry wit – emerged with a striking, brand new nickname for dad: *'The Balding Eagle', he* belters out! An American dear friend of mine in her early fifties, in an effort to control her diet eats as many vegetables as she possibly could lay her hands upon, at a breakfast seating. She confided in me recently, that her children nicknamed her such variant of names ranging from *'celery', 'cucumber'* and *'radishes'* to *'lettuce-ball', 'cabbage',* and *'carrot-bug'!*

Here's the point I am making: *praise-giving genders an endearment, a closeness and a bonding!*

Lesson #3 ~ Praise, before criticism:
Before you criticize a friend, always make it a point of emphasis; first, to praise their achievements and positive impact. Before you criticize anyone, be honest and candid enough to share your own mistakes! Call attention to peoples' mistakes *not* with a halogen spot-lamp in hand, but indirectly – maybe with a wicker oil-lamp!

Before you criticize a friend, bear in mind to avoid the pit of cynicism. Do not become overt-critical; if you do, you risk losing that friend. Unarguably, they may have caused potential emotional hurt, *yet* you must allow them the privilege to soul-search and possibly arrive at the destination of penitence. Our western civilization counter-teaches the doctrine of grace – the very doctrine at the core of Father God's heart of restoration.

Never throw anyone a sucker punch!

If after having lovingly confronted them, they re-gain insight, backtrack and apologize, you've won them. Daddy God demands *you* forgive them – that He too may forgive you!

Additionally, the merciful God demands even more of you; He requests that you find every means possible to restore and nurture your broken friendships/relationships to wholeness – with a renewed vision and passion to probably attaining a healthier relationship, than at the first. Make room for restoration to occur. Anticipate it. Welcome the opportunity to restore and heal – with open hands!

Lesson #4 ~ Be ready to apologize – and mean every word of your apology:

Humble yourself – and be not piqued in pride. Once you've recognized your error, tender an unreserved apology – and mean every word of it. The three-worded sentence *'I am sorry'*, if rendered in true spirit of sorrowfulness of heart always works wonders!

We do not apologize only because we were caught by the arm, but rather, because our hearts are genuinely sorry!

Similarly, we do not apologize *only* when in the wrong. An apology would be tenable if in retrospect, we arrived at a realization of what our actions, reactions or in-actions had caused in the "build-up" processes that had eventually led to the offender's "outlandish" outburst. It's nothing different from you owning up to your insurance company and *the Motor Insurance Bureau,* the panic your action "cutting" in front of the other driver had caused them – which action had left them with no other alternative than maneuvering or veering into your driver's side. We agree that to be the proper thing to do, don't we?

Abasing yourself before a friend, whom you have misguided, misled or caused to err is an indication of your willingness to succor their emotional anguish – sharing in their emotional overload. Nothing can possibly better graphically depict how much you value their friendship's worth.

Again, apologize *not* only when you are in the wrong. Morals and ethics demand that you apologize *even* when you seem to be in the right, but may have been misconceived or misunderstood. Doing this automatically douses sparks of argument that may potentially result in an uncontrollable flame. The Father's heart commands us to *"follow peace with all men, and holiness,"* without which no one shall experience, encounter or see the Lord.[1]

Kindly let your apology be born out of a sincere *"godly sorrow and repentance."*[2] In their growing up years, my *five friends* noticed my apology as cynical, if my use of the three-worded sentence had preceded a rebuke or a correction; an offender knew trouble was brewing when with a stern look, I had started with a sentence such as: *"I am sorry you were a little bit un-wise in your doings ..."*

Once you have apologized, ask God's Holy Spirit for grace

to enable you *not* repeat the same offensive act. Also, be mindful to ask the Father for the heart of the one you have offended to be willing to receive your apology.

The Power of Your Choice in Friendship

"A friend is a person with whom I may be sincere. Before him, I may think aloud."
(Ralph Waldo Emerson, U.S poet and essayist)

Who is a true friend?

According to Ralph Waldo Emerson, a true friend is a person with whom you may dare to be sincere. In other words, a true friend simply is someone with whom you have been afforded the luxury of being your *very* self! Whilst many rehearse their thought-patterns prior to a dialog/discussion; according to Emerson, you wouldn't need to entertain the fear of being remonstrated by a true friend. Thus, you could afford to *"think aloud"* in their presence.

Charles C. Colton, the English clergyman and satirist of the 18th century said: *"Friendships often end in love; but love in friendship – never."*

Believe this certainty: *your* choice in friendship has *your* destiny at stake. Our friends mirror us, and we, them! Our personalities will be tempered and molded alongside the shades and hues of our friends' – or the group of people we have chosen to surround ourselves with. The wisest man that ever lived, Solomon, in one of his writings had penned: *"He who walks [as a companion] with wise men is wise, but he who associates with [self-confident] fools is [a fool himself] and shall smart for it."*[3]

God's Word has something pertinent to say of the choice Prince Amnon – one of the sons of King David – had made in friendship:

> *"But Amnon had a friend, whose name was Jonadab, the son of Shimeah David's brother: and Jonadab was a very subtil man."*
>
> 2 Samuel 13:3

That archaic biblical word above, *'subtil'*, was the same word that metamorphosed into today's modern English word *'subtle'*. It is a very strong word.

So what does it mean to be subtle?

The *Concise Dictionary, 21ˢᵗ Century Edition*, offers these definitions to the word "subtle":

- *"not immediately obvious or comprehensible;*

- *difficult to detect or analyze;*

- *marked by or requiring mental acuteness or ingenuity;*

- *cunning or wily; and*

- *operating or executed in secret."*

What are you operating in secrecy? What deal have you been involved in, offered or cut?

Whatever it is, be rest assured that *if* you continue to make advancement on the momentary gains which subtlety brings, you will certainly be brought to shame, sorrow and ruin! An ancient wise guy by the name of Zophar wrote in the oldest book ever known to mankind:

"Knowest thou not this of old, since man was placed upon earth,

That the triumphing of the wicked is short, and the joy of the hypocrite, but for a moment?"

Job 20:4-5

A man had obtained British citizenship via the route of an *Indefinite Leave to Remain* in the United Kingdom when, in reality, he had *not* fulfilled the requirements for eligibility to remain. Hardly had he lived a total of five weeks of the mandated total of five years required by the law to become lawfully eligible.

At the onset, he had applied for the *Higher Skilled Migrant Program* status/visa – and with that had entered the country. Nevertheless, he had an ulterior motive: understudy the loopholes in the system – and extort them!

He soon found one!

He had discovered that the *HSMP* regulations allowed one to float a company that rendered basic economic services, thus enhancing the British economy. Additionally, he had also soon found other crooked men with same disposition as his. They had helped him "hire" an address, open a bank account and remit taxes from overseas. All was looking pretty.

He had actually flown in into the United Kingdom, in the first year of his visa in order to make his case look more plausible. Since he'd been on a genuine entry permit, all he needed do was fly in and out of the U.K. at wish, in a bid to convince the U.K Border Patrol of his *live* status – whilst ensuring that the immigration authorities in his departing country did *not* record his exit from their departure port. It was an easier plot because the *United Kingdom Border Patrol* requirements did *not* necessitate traveling documents be stamped on departure *from* the United Kingdom! This continues, to be one of the weaknesses in our immigration "system."

Towards the expiration of his original five-year-valid passport which contained the original *HSMP* entry permit; in the fifth year, this dubious person had flown in, this time, to hatch *his* plot. *It was easy; he would declare under oath, his passport, as lost!* He'd found a solicitor firm in London through which he'd sworn a false oath of a lost passport. That in place, he'd proceeded to falsely report to the *Metropolitan Police* of same "loss" attested by an oath – and had obtained a crime reference number. He'd secured a brand new passport from his native country's embassy in the capital – and when he'd presented his papers to the *Home Office*, he'd not only gained accreditation of worthiness, but also the sympathy of the erstwhile officials, expressing sympathy for his lost document!

Soon, he'd filed immigration papers for his wife and five children – two of whom really, are a distant niece and nephew. Being of a depraved mind as he was, he'd found a way to falsify genotype/paternity test outcomes, bribing his way through a government accredited medical test center in his corrupt home country.

All had worked well for him until someday he had been involved in a minor road accident whereupon his furnishing of documents, it had been discovered that there had been a deft touch to his driving license. Somehow, his birth date had rung a bell with the right quarters; *DVLA* had launched an extensive investigation – so also had the insurance company.

Soon, tall guys in shiny black helmets had begun knocking on his door for investigative questioning. Fraud investigation officers from the insurance company had also followed suit. It was like a Domino-effect; the *Home Office* had finally requested him to re-appear at Croydon with his and his family members' documents! It had been their twelfth year possessing the red passport and living 'peacefully' in the United Kingdom. However, once the *Home Office* had concluded her inquiries and had found misappropriations and illegality in their backgrounds, he and his family had been deprived of citizenship – and deported!

Now, the key person this errant man lacked was a true friend with whom he could have been afforded the pleasure to "think aloud"; someone who would have stopped him right in his tracks, in the conception stage of his subtlety!

Amnon – as in this true story shared above – didn't have a confidant in Jonadab whom he'd relied upon as his best friend.

What a pity!

The Power of Counsel in Friendship

"Where no counsel is the people fall: but in the multitude of counsellors, there is safety."

Proverbs 11:14

"The heart of the prudent getteth knowledge; and the ear of the wise seeketh knowledge."

Proverbs 18:15

A couple of names ring a sonorous bell whenever the issue of either *not* seeking or receiving proper counsel before embarking upon decisive actions crops up.

First, General Gideon had made the costliest mistake of his career when both he and the Israeli Council had *not* received counsel from Father God but rather had consented to the requests of the Gibeonites in acquiescence, sparing them from destruction.[1] Two days later, their request had been discovered as an hoax; an irrecoverable farce! Israel had entered into an irrevocable covenant with them, a covenant that would eventually prove costlier to the entire nation, a few years down their history lane.

Second, Rehoboam, King Solomon's son had surrounded himself with peers from his university days as counselors, upon his ascension onto the throne of Israel following the death of his father. As a mere formality, he had consulted with the sound counsel of *"the old men"* that had helped his predecessor maintain peace and achieve a strong, vibrant, prosperous economy! However, the young jolly king had disgracefully shunned the sages' words. He'd delivered an unwise speech that had promised to double taxes, increase interest rates, reduce pay – and crack down heavily on anyone who dared dissent.[5] Following his ill-advised speech, the Nation of Israel had quickly spiraled into chaos and revolt. She'd ended being split up; ir-reconcilably, into two kingdoms: the *Northern* and *Southern Kingdoms*.

You have seen from very ancient stories what influence friends' counsels wield upon lives! Lessons learned in retrospect – contrary to popular view – may *not* be wisdom, after all! Each action we execute is a seed planted. Seeds are renowned for their perennial, successful afforestation campaigns!

Take for instance, King David's paralyzing inability to resist the adulterous thought to desire Mrs. Bathsheba Uriah when it had festered in his heart, that lazy spring afternoon. The king had yielded – having embarked on a course that would forever tip the scales against him, his children, his kingdom and his beloved country, Israel.

'Uumm; if only king David hadn't lusted after Bathsheba on that fine, spring day; many errors would have been averted', we would think! Well, that is only *a* blessing of hindsight.

Foresight, however, takes positive accounts of premonition. *Foresight* would have instructed the king to nip the evil thought to commit adultery in the bud, as soon as it had flashed on his mind's screen. *"Replace that idle picture of a bathing naked woman in your mind"* he must have been duly warned, *"with that of positive busy-ness at the warfront – after all, the war front was where you ought to have been!"*

"Okay, what have all these got to do with me?" you ask!

I will answer you.

If you are struggling with a bad habit, an addiction or an evil thought, you actually do have at your advantage the double benefits foresight and hindsight do offer.

Foresight helps you effect pragmatic checkpoints – one of which is the luxury of surrounding yourself with two or three sincere friends, who can offer you free quality advice, "watch your back" – and with whom you will feel secure being accountable unto, in order to avert potential lurking trouble. Remember, in the multitude of counselors, there is safety!

Hindsight on the other hand provides ample stories and teachings you read in the Word of God, or hear of others' lives. Often, these become great reference tools. Never ignore the huge advantages both foresight and hindsight offer.

Ammon, like the lustful King David had also taken the first wrong step; he had discounted the power of godly choice in friendship. He'd ended up having an incestuous carnal relationship with Tamar, his half-sister! Absalom, Tamar's big brother had eventually murdered him a couple of years later. The bounteous yields of the sin-seed planted had *not* terminated in that field of blood:

Absalom's gross misconduct against his father, King David had eventually led to his own death!

Remember these wise words of King Solomon:

> *"The heart of the prudent getteth knowledge; and the ear of the wise seeketh knowledge."*
>
> Proverbs 18:15

My Counsel

In the spirit of fraternity of the same paternity, permit me to counsel you concerning the various issues bordering on *'keeper'* friendships and healthy relationships.

• *How far is 'too far'?*

If this is the question agitating your mind: *'How far is too far?'*; then, *'far'* in any situation is *"too far"*, when anyone involved in the friendship/relationship has deliberately set aside, bluntly ignored, intentionally disregarded or flagrantly transgressed acceptable limits. For instance, a motorist doing *30 m.p.h* in a *20 m.p.h* restriction-zone has flagrantly flaunted the law; he/she has transgressed!

Simply defined, *"transgression" is a total disregard of, setting light the law; or, going beyond the set boundaries.*

Boundaries are set by the countries and states of the world, counties and cities, corporations and individuals!

Do you have any boundaries?

For the Christ follower, things would be deemed as having progressed "too far" if any counselor suggests contrary to

the written Word of God as enunciated in the Holy Bible!
Counsel of such nature directly leads to compromising
situations. You must *not* avail yourself to anyone, to be led
or coerced into compromising situations. Be re-assured,
there are no grey areas in the Word of God; it either is
"God did say" or "God did *not* say"!

- ***I am in a committed relationship, can't we romance
  each other – and possibly pet?***
An age-long adage instructs a famished, erstwhile eater
of a pot of hot porridge to approach the bowlful with
much patience and carefulness so as not to sustain burns
to the mouth, tongue and lips. In all likelihood, romance
prepares the way for foreplay, if not nipped in the bud.
That is as best as I could most honestly render it.

You probably have listened to one of your closest lady/
girlfriends begin expressing her pain and disappointment
in a statement often ridden with guilt, such as: "I *fell*
pregnant …"

The emphasis is on the word *"fell."*

When a female "falls" pregnant, she literally means she was
involved with a man/boyfriend in a romance that had led
to foreplay – and past the point of self-restraints on either
party. She had discovered she had conceived – and had
chosen the wiser option to keep her baby and not abort the
pregnancy. We should commend her wise, latter decision.

In most cultures of the world, in olden times – English
culture inclusive – a baby conceived out of wedlock
earned the *"b"* word which I possibly can't complete

writing. In those *Dark Ages*, such babies were either abandoned, given up for adoption – or gained upon by the Social Services!

On the contrary, in today's age of enlightenment, you would think that we have gained upon societal levels of expectations. But *no!* Rather, levels of expectations regarding morality, ethics and spirituality have continuously slipped, further and further below the *status quo!* Nevertheless, the Christ follower must always remember that our heavenly Father had it spelled in black-and-white, as unambiguously as possible: *"Thou shalt not commit adultery or [fornication]."*[6]

I have always counseled that *true love* is gentle and patient. True love will persevere, endure and wait – no matter how long it takes! You should *not* under-estimate the power of a true love. Neither should you equate *lust* with God's Father-heart love; they two, are incomparable!

Furthermore, I counsel Christ-lovers to agree, setting a healthy "Abiding Love Boundary Declaration", just of this sort:

> *"We solemnly bind ourselves by this oath before the Father of love that there shall exist no amorous, sensuous touching; no petting – nor indeed any involvement whatsoever of the physical members until OUR wedding night."*

If you concur to my proposal, ratify it right here before the Father, His holy angels – and yourselves. Append your signatures on the dotted lines, below:

------------------------------   ------------------------------
(*Lover A*).   (*Lover B*).

Congratulations. This is your first step unto *your* consecration, both!

I know of *not* a few couples who started their marital journeys together based on this disciplined but rewarding, joint-decision commitment to sanctity. Their joint-will during courtship, they later testified, further strengthened and deepened their mutual trust and respect in marriage – even when they had *not* been physically present with each other.

Conversely, I do also know quite a few couples whose essential trust in and respect of each other *never* stayed clean, past the second – or at most, the third year of their marriages. (You probably can rightly guess the reason for their distrust and doubts).

Hear me very well: *every* season in your marriage is a crucial time you must diligently attend unto. The first two or three years in *any* marriage, however, are the most critical period; when the depths of the "in-love" feelings are most agonizingly "sounded" by the sharpest sonars of individual knowledge about life and the application of principles that guarantee results!

Some marital commitments and depths, you will be surprised to find out, have *not* stood against the tides. Some sharper sonar of affairs, flings and infidelities have tested some marriages at those delicate first two or three years of some couples' bonding. They had *not* measured a fathom!

The outcomes of these ferocious sonar tests?

Wearisomeness and a string of disappointments!

For these disappointed couples, the painful flashback memories to *their* intimate infidelity moments whilst they dated/courted were always watershed points of references in latter emotional pains and anguish. If you care to listen more raptly to their confessions, such statements as: *"All he/she wanted was my money ..."*, *"I felt entirely used; now I feel worthless"*, *"He/She will do it with someone else, besides me, too!"* *etcetera* are characteristically dominant, as they reflect!

I apologize, if my counsel of abstinence from romance during courtship sounds offensive to your thought-style; but I have your utmost well-being at heart! I do *not* want your emotions hurt and damaged; your memories, tainted! Neither does *the* Heavenly Father.

Similarly, a Christ follower ought *never* to give a second thought to considering entering into a serious friendship/relationship with a member of the opposite sex who is *not* of the household of faith. If your fast-forwarded thought is laden with expectation such as: *'I will convert him once we are in a relationship,'* – be careful!

The Father heart of the Creator has *not* left us destitute of guidance and instruction, which are always for our good. His Word counsels us: *"Be not unequally yoked together with unbelievers."*[7] Of course, as colleagues, mates and associates, we may be friendly to relate. No one should ostracize him/herself from his community or sphere of influence because of his/her faith; but *only* plutonic friendliness, that's as far as it should go!*[8]

- ***Isn't it OK for a woman to 'chase' her choice man?***
In the *Singles* seminars that I have ministered at, the question
kept re-occurring: *"Isn't it OK for a woman to chase her choice man?"*
I understand and share your concern. I am aware that
the statistical birth ratio of the female to the male is
much higher – and that the female, in general, has a
slightly longer lifespan than her counterpart, the male.
*Notwithstanding, it is the male who has heard the voice of the Lord
in clear guidance and direction who seeks and finds the woman to
be his companion!*

Not vice, versa!

Our world-system may teach us otherwise, but a
daughter of Zion does not 'chase' a man of her
choice. If she does, she leaves herself vulnerable to a
consequential result of *his* toying with *her* emotions.[9]
Please don't misunderstand me; you may *send him a
godly smile* or *a wink,* once or twice, to get him to notice
you – and there's absolutely nothing wrong in doing
that! Bless you if your glances catch his fancy. If he
doesn't take notice of you, simply let go; pray, and then
"eye" someone else. (If the female was the one that
first received a confirmation from the Lord, she would
never "eye" another. She remains resolute, firm, quietly
waiting for *her* man to make the necessary move – which
when he makes, she acquiesces unto, without *any* waste
of time!)

Some other times however, when both gentleman and
lady are *not* Christ-followers but are deeply in love; the
girl has been emboldened to propose marriage to him if

he has been unnecessarily shy.

- ***If a man approaches a woman in the name of the Lord!***

If a man approaches a woman and says to her: *"God has spoken to me about you becoming my wife";* thank God for his boldness. Additionally, ask him to accord you space and time so you also may seek the face of the Lord. God's face, alone, you should seek; no one else's opinion is *primarily* relevant at this stage. Not even those of your momma or *bestie!* (Grannies most times, have been spot on; their wisdom, incomparable. But at this crucial stage, you seek God's opinion, first!)

Now, some ladies invite their girlfriend along in order to help "size-up" a potential suitor when meeting for a date. While this is not intrinsically wrong, their prime motives may be suspect. Similarly, not a few ladies deliberately invite their friends along on-line, to "befriend" a potential suitor so as to help stalk/keep track of his on-line activities. Her best-friends – unbeknown to the suitor – have been surreptitiously charged to "tempt", "lure" or "draw out" his real intents and feelings. Good on you, both!

Sometimes, treacherous *"besties"* have won – and defected loyalties, and turned on their bestie with a beastly fierceness! Remember, *"Whatsoever is not of faith is sin"* (Romans 14:23). Scripture categorically teaches every *person* to be fully persuaded in their own minds![10]

The young Prophet from Judah
Permit me to share with you possible consequence(s)

of willful disobedience – even after having personally established a confirmation from the mouth of the Lord.

The story involved a young prophet *"out of Judah"*. The Lord asked him to travel to Bethel – and prophesy against the altar in that city. Once he accomplished his mission, he was specifically instructed to depart the city and *not* return for *any* reason whatsoever!

However, it occurred that on his way from Bethel, a renowned *"older prophet"* lied to him in the name of the Lord, against the backdrop of *his* original personal conviction. So, he agreed to a detour. It turned out to be a deadly detour. He ended paying the ultimate fatal price.[11]

Thus, when any person visits a minister and requests counsel, wisdom behooves such minister to cross-examine them: *"What has the Lord said to you, personally?"* Anything short of this may justify an accusation index finger being pointed at such minister/spiritual counselor as a counseling error. (Notice, I said, *"may"*, with a strong emphasis!)

Listen. If you do *not* wish to be mauled by the hungry lions loitering on *'Disobedient-Destiny Highway I-666'*; then, a mutually agreeable time should be set during which the lady that has received a proposal from a potential suitor *would* seek the face of the Lord *personally,* to inquire from His mouth, what His perfect will is, for her marital life!

More befitting, they *both* should agree to set time apart from each other, to seek the Lord! Between three and seven days at an instant, may be deemed appropriate – even though, no one may be able to specifically advise how long or short, your consultation with the Father could eventually take.

The onus of accepting or refusing the man's proposal essentially rests upon the lady. A gentleman at no point in time, puts her under duress, stress or pressure of any kind!

Lady, if you do *not* feel convinced about his proposal at the present, because of "circumspectly circumstance(s)" that surround either of you, calm him down and tell him exactly what you *see*. Re-assure him of your love but let him be aware of those issues that needed pragmatic working out upon, first, before you *will* re-consider his proposal for marriage. Stay strongly connected, but *you* also stay supportive and calm! He is *not* going to even attempt to "run about" if he's *the* one assigned unto you by the Creator Father God!

If on the other hand, you knew within your innermost being, this man isn't *the* one for you, godliness and righteousness compel you to let him know as soon as possible.

Do not "moor" him!

Mooring has been used by indiscreet ladies since time immemorial. They "moor" with the gross aim of manipulation to gain emotional control over men, mete out denial, rejection, retaliation of some sort or inflict an emotional pain. Your outward demeaning may look cool like a cucumber and as irresistible as an angel, but dare I tell you the stark truth? Your act, simply, is the devil's witchcraft's ace!

Some other times, God's Holy Spirit may have revealed

ahead of the suitor's approach, to the lady: *"So-and-so is your husband!"*

In such instances, the lady would be astute to contain the revelation *within*; first, until *he* – the suitor – lends a voice of conviction to her revelation!

Contrariwise, if the Lord subsequently confirms to the lady – particularly in the negative to the man's proposal – before the expiration of the time agreed upon by both for prayers, there's no point *'stalling'* him. She should call him up, and both honestly and frankly tell him *'in love'* what word she has received of the Lord. The lady should *not* hold on to him, as a possible *"second highest bidder"*. *You* are a daughter of the King – and *not* an auction item. Hallelujah!

If a lady has asked a man to give her time to seek God's face, the guy should be magnanimous enough to *'give space'*. He ought also to be seeking the face of the Lord at such a time; praying for clear counsel from the mouth of the Lord for the girl, so that she would *not* say *'yes'*, when she indeed meant to say *'no'* – and *vice versa*.

A godly suitor is patient at such an important junction of destiny as this. Godly counsel bids him "wait". He must avoid serial dating or web browsing for alternatives to the one he'd approached with his love. Righteous men do *not* second-guess the exact word from the mouth of the Lord!

- *Issues regarding same sex relationship and other sexual deviation-types:*

81

I received an email in 2006, from one of the readers of *PULSE On-line*, our ministry's free on-line publication found on our website *www.harvestways.org*

The writer – an eighteen year old female from Alabama, a southern U.S. state had asked: *"OK, Rev.; What do you make of same sex relationship?"*

I had replied that the Father Creator-God did *not* ordain homosexual/lesbian or gay relationships, irrespective of what government's policy, the media, the magazines – and celebrities may want us to believe. This *forever* remains my stance on this issue. (Please, read Romans 1:18-32).

She'd eventually subscribed to our free teaching materials – and had begun reading and meditating!

Gradually, correspondence had become frequent between us; she'd also grown more confident to be able to ask us various other questions which had been promptly replied.

About eight months later, she'd written:

"Dear Reverend Sammy,

I thank you for your most honest teaching of the word of God. I have read and digested your materials in the wee hours of the night, with much pain and agony of heart ... It has been an intense battle! Last week, I made up my mind that I had had enough ...

I said the little prayer at the end of the teaching – and felt an inexplicable overpowering presence of God's washing and cleansing come all over me.

Thank you for being faithful to your calling; please keep teaching the undiluted word of God."

Signed,

Sammie.
(Not her real name!)

More correspondence soon evolved into phone calls that had centered on her newfound faith in Christ. It emerged that Sammie had suffered the guilt, condemnation, depression and confusion associated with being involved in a same-sex relationship. Despite the 4 444 miles that separated us, prayers had been raised – and she'd been advised to attend a local church.

She had – and had begun to grow in her love for the Lord!

In 2009, Sammie met the man of her dreams – and both got married. They remain happily married; our ministry is still very much in contact with that young family!

I shared this young lady's triumphant story over lesbianism because I am well aware that there are some of you in similar situation as she had been, wanting to break lose – yet undergoing tremendous struggle and helplessness. Like an addict yearning to come clean and break free, homosexuality has you in its clutches, bound!

Should you *really* want to come to terms with the true love of the Heavenly Father God, your true identity and sexuality, help is available in the Blood of the Lamb.

"So God created man in his own image, in the image of God created he him; male and female created he them."

Genesis 1:27

You're *not* a mere creature, rather; you're a creature of His intent. There is no mix-up in the heavenly Father's design of you – neither did He endorse *any* kind of sexual deviation or pervasion as in any wise good, for you!

Commonest Sexual Deviation Types

Permit me to share with you, some of the commonest sexual perversions you must avoid:

• *The L.G.B.T:*

The confusion lesbianism, gay (homosexuality), bi-sexuality/curiosity and the trans-gendered have brought – and continue to promulgate in sexual dis-orientations of our teeming youth populations can no more be labeled as "in the minority". Yet, God's word clearly warns against engaging in any of these depraved practices of the *'LGBT'* (Read *Romans 1:18-28*).

• *Pornography and Cyber-sex:*

You may argue with your conscience, but pornography and cyber-sex closely associated with rape are the commonest sexual epidemics of this day and age; yet, the holy Father God strongly advises that you stay away from lustful passions and debauchery. Not only is watching porn condemned but even the encouragement, approval and applause of those engaged in the pervasive acts are equally reproved by the holy God of Heaven.

• *Incest:*
Incestuous relationships take place between family members and blood relations. It is an aberration from God's divine will regarding sexuality.

• *Bestiality:*
Engaging in the sex act with animals or pets is a defiling grievous sexual sin. Bestiality bestializes the human soul. Fondling and petting pets are also condemned.

• *Uncleanliness:*
Having sex with a menstruating woman is one classical example of uncleanness. Gross, dirty, impure thoughts; wild provocative talk, heavy suggestive breathing mimicking orgasms and tempestuous alluring acts on telephone or Skype sex are labeled as unclean, by the holy God of Heaven.

• *Necrophilism:*
Having sex – or harboring the desire to have sex – with a lifeless being initiates into and binds your soul with the world of the abhorrent demonic spirits!

You see, the Father heart of God has set us healthy boundaries in the use of sex and the expression of our sexuality purely because of the love He has for us!

I do not desire to see any of my children hurt while playing in our garden; thus, I deliberately set them healthy boundaries or confines within which they could safely explore. Exploration outside of those healthy safety limits becomes an issue of concern to me as *their* Father!

These above, definitely, are *not* all there exists of sexual deviations and pervasions. However, if you have been struggling with *any* of these sexual dysfunctions; again, I assure you, help is available! Call upon God; own up before Him. Begin your deliverance and emancipation, today.

In some instances, those demonic spirits that bring about these demonic cravings to secure such strongholds will not leave *until* you have requested the helps of some truly anointed servants of God. I am not talking of exorcism here, rather, I am treading the line of thought of Apostle James who encourages *you* to call for spiritual re-enforcement in a God-ordained spiritual hierarchy *(James 5:14-16)*.

Call upon the name of the Lord, with other anointed servants of God who will closely walk with you through your deliverance process. Do *not* fight alone. Ask for – and receive the help that the loving Father offers!

Dating a Divorcee

I do *not* want you misconceived thinking that I am trying to tag upon you a label – if you are divorced and ready to date. Heaven commissioned me however, to deliver *the* wholesome doctrine. As someone who has undergone the painful process of the death of a marriage, you must be ready to give an honest account of yourself, *anytime!*

The following seven pertinent questions, therefore, you need to ask your divorcee-lover:

1. Inquire about the circumstances that led to their

divorce:

If they have been divorced – at least once, perfect reasoning demands that you inquire, first and foremost; the circumstances surrounding their divorce(s). As you engage in your inquiries, it is *not* unlikely that you would *not* be told an impartial story.[12] You'd be smart to be very patient to learn, with time, *the true* story!

You'd also do well to ascertain that the divorce paper(s) they claim to possess were genuinely issued by the court. Additionally, clarify in a "matter-of-factly" mode whether they intend to be restored to their *ex*. (Do *not* be so naïve; you would be surprised at what sordid acts of foolishness transpire between "amicable ex's" – particularly if they have maintained regular contacts with each other!)

2. *Custodial/Contact-time arrangement with children:*

A major factor often bringing "amicable ex's" into proximity of each other is 'contact time' with their *minor* children – particularly, if they share custody!

If they sired children who are *minors*, it will do you much good to learn of court orders, pronouncements and legal arrangements regarding custody/parental visitation rights. Discuss into the minutest details, listening with open-ears what such arrangements spell for you, were you to get married to them. Some parties agree to visit in your new home together with you being there/out. Some others agree to *drop 'n pick* children at the door! Yet a few others agree to meet at Contact Centers – and some critical ones, at the Police Station.

I do *not* know which option may best work for you,

but you have a stake in the matter, to negotiate with your divorcee-mother/father-lover!

3. Inquire about their current health-status:

Anyone above the mid-thirties' who has been through the stress of at least a divorce has a moderate likelihood to be on *a* prescription medication – even if it is a rare, mere analgesic!

Don't be fooled by external good looks; ask pertinent questions about the state of their physical health. *"Are they on prescription medicine?"* If they are, *"Are they faithfully following physician's prescriptions?"*

Some people fail to dote on their medications on intent. They cite various excuses ranging from forgetfulness to allergies; to: *"The medication just induces weight-gain or drowsiness, and I just plain loathe the thought of being subjected to that rut, for the rest of my life"*; to bizarre, unsubstantiated claims of a spiritual healing when such healing has not manifested in the physical!

Well, here's the truth: if his/her attitude is going to be selfish, he/she might just as well get prepared to spend the rest of his/her life single, not involving an innocent party in his/her possibly imminent tragedy!

"Presumption" is a word too costly to afford! True love defies sicknesses and ill health, but *you* reserve the right to privy knowledge of his/her state of health before you tie the knot. Denying you of that right is plain, dubious!

Some men are sterile – and thus can never have children, medically speaking. Another middle-aged, impotent male is yet "goading on" a late-twenties' lady high on hope of marrying, bearing children and raising a family together with him. Some older woman who has had an hysterectomy *op* performed is heavily in love with a younger dude who desires to raise a family with her.

Please would you be kind and honest enough to declare your states of being?

The truth is, if they loved you enough – and could afford to pay the *price for love*, they would still be with you, despite your overwhelming, mind-boggling secrets locked within the recesses of your heart accessible to no one but only *you!*

4. Similarly, raise relevant inquiries about the health of their finance and spending patterns:

Watch carefully over time, their financial prudence, or the lack of it! Money and debt matters constitute a significant part in the health of any relationship; so, *ask:*

- *How much debt they do owe – and what are the repayment terms?*

- *Do they have a mortgage – and would they wish to transfer/ share ownership with you; are they re-mortgaging, any time soon?*

- *Was their car fully paid, purchased on Finance or on an Hire Purchase Agreement?*

- *Do they possess a home insurance – and how does its payment affect you were you both to get married?*

Ask, ask – and ask enough questions in order to bring before the heavenly Father, issues that may likely bear direct impact

Appreciable Gifts

upon your relationship – were you to get married!

> *"Ask, and it shall be given you; seek, and ye shall find; knock, and it shall be opened unto you:*
>
> *For every one that asketh receiveth; and he that seeketh, findeth; and to him that knocketh it shall be opened."*
>
> Matthew 7: 7-8

Father God would rather that you had potent knowledge and understanding of whom your soul desires in marriage beforehand, than getting married, only to discover a world of hidden varieties. Do *not* set yourself up for a marital failure!

5. Inquire about the state of their spiritual health:
Ask questions about their spiritual life. Do they attend a church? Would they be willing that you visit with them, on a church fellowship day? Are they a volunteering member of such church's/ministry's sub-group?

When people have *not* volunteered to join ministerial sub-groups in churches, it is an indicator to an inexcusable very busy work-schedule, a subtle pride problem, or a glaring insubordinate spirit, unwilling to submit to the local spiritual authority.

Ask questions about their *daily* spiritual walk with the Father! Ask them to share the portion of scriptures the Father spoke to them from, *today!* Trade prayer points. Keep a journal of answered prayers! If they lag behind in any of these spiritual exercises – and request help, at least you'd know how to encourage them! If they seem

90

not to need your help, you'd equally be aware of *who* and *what* you're letting yourself into!

If they do *not* attended church having no obvious prohibitive factor such as being homebound by a physical infirmity, their avoidance of fellowship with the *Body* must indicate the presence of a deeper spiritual hurt in their relationship with the heavenly Father! (Same thing applies unto an avowed child of God bound by the spirit of pornography: it is also an outer evidence of an inner brokenness and a lack of spiritual intimacy with the Father's love).

6. Ask questions about their emotional, psychological, moral and ethical states of being:

Inquire what their opinions of social issues, are, generally. If you have children whom you're hoping to raise jointly, begin early to raise questions bordering on boundaries: who the spokes-person disciplinarian would be – or is it going to be a joint-discipline enforcement venture between you both? Gain perspective of their positions, for example, on issues as '*Up until what time your teenagers are expected back in the house were they to go out; where could or couldn't they go – and with who or who not with?*'

Tread other borderline, social issues carefully; for example, what *genre of music, DVD's, TV shows* and computer games would pass your acceptance censorship-limits? *Internet rules: its availability, children's rationed online availability hours per week and its child-protective settings;* social life standards such as *wine consumption – or lack of it; partying – or no partying, acceptable* cum *unacceptable language/ slangs* and, last but not the least, *dress-codes etcetera!*

Begin in earnest, to inquire – and be ready to accommodate their opinions. Most of all, gear up to compromise, healthily!

7. Ask if they have/have not a job or a business that brings in a stream of legal earnings?

If they have not at present a means of supporting their livelihood, inquire closely, what active, tackling measures they are adopting – or have adopted – to address this issue? Are they busy seeking employment or not? Are they starting a business?

8. Questions about their character-references:

Additional to asking pertinent questions, a divorcee's character references over the years and months – as the case may be – should also be sought from both 'close quarters' and 'far quarters' – given their permission.

If however, they deny your request to seek references, there must be cogent reasons for their obstruction; you would be smart to desire those reasons be brought to light, in a mood of an understandable, congenial discussion!

Again, ask questions – and open *both* your physical and spiritual eyes and ears in clear observations and perceptions.

Above all, watch *over time*, for evidence – or lack of it, of a healed heart!

SMH, Smiling!

SMH is an online term/slang that translates *"Shaking my head!"*

You probably are shaking your head in disbelief to the varied requests as I have enumerated, smiling! I would strongly implore you to *not* to be offended if anyone demands of you, any of them. Rather, be bold, glad and ready to furnish them answers to their requests. Your eagerness and readiness to "reveal your true worth" would indeed unveil the extent of the preparatory measures to re-invent yourself you've taken, over the years, since you've been single.

Your thoughtful, careful approach to this new love prospect is akin to a successful new marriage so you would indeed *not* have to repeat the mistakes of the past.

Requesting such "evidences" from any person who had been divorced but is contemplating re-marrying should be deemed as purposeful on intent; a too-good-to-miss hint of their desire to pursue with you, an active relationship that could in all possibility result in a marriage commitment! There is a lot to gain being honest, sincere and real!

After the expiration of a couple of years of loneliness – or more fruitless dating and searching efforts, divorcees, in some cases retrospectively begin to rationalize the thoughts that probably working through their dead marriage could indeed have been a better and cheaper option than divorce. In some miraculous cases, love has been re-ignited in the same couple. In some worse scenarios, divorcees have re-married only to notice that they secretly miss their ex's; *very* badly! They live in silent regret – bearing a huge burden of an eternal sadness!

Whatever Your Burden

There is no person on the face of the earth who is burden-free. We are all laden – to variably different extents! Nevertheless, here's a piece of *Goodnews*: there avails a Burden-bearer. A strong-shouldered, willing, Burden-bearer. A Helper-friend, able and ready to help lift our weights and carry our burdens! Kindly permit me to facilitate the introduction to you, of this *new* Friend. Scripture refers to Him as that *"friend that sticks closer than a brother"* (Proverbs 18:24).

This friend is *not* just another friend; indeed, He is *the* embodiment of love! He is *not* a figment of some wild imagination, He is ever-present. He never leaves you alone to tackle the cruel realities underlying life's burdens. He stays to offer His help!

His name is Jesus Christ!

At the mention of this name, I may have aroused your deepest emotions. You may not have been a believer in Him. In fact, you may in no way desire His friendship; yet, I am persuaded by the Father's Spirit to believe that you are *"ordained"* of Him as His friend! Just by virtue of you reading this book thus far without any external force or coercion, I *know* that His seal of friendship is upon you! Listen to the voice of *your* Sacred Friend speak to *your* spirit:

> *"You have not chosen me, but I have chosen you and ordained you ..."*

> John 15:16

Says He, emphatically, *"I have called you friend!"*

You are probably saying to yourself: *'O.K., Reverend Sammy; you don't know how bruised, battered and damaged I have become!'*

For you, there is a *"balm in Gilead."*[13] This *Healer Balm* soothes, binds and heals the wounded inner recesses. He is called Immanuel.[14]

The Wonderful.

The Counselor.

The Mighty God.

The Prince of Peace.

The everlasting Father.

The One whose increase of Kingdom and Government of peace has no end.[15] He wants to gain access into companionship with you – *right now!*

Allow Him.

Receive His peace into your heart; it dominates the longest, darkest hours when all else is none else!

Summary of Chapter 3

1.) In life, never had any two pathways crossed by mere happenstance. *Either* the Creator-Father or His stark opponent, Satan orchestrated *your* friendly prospect. Your duty it is to discover who the *orchestrator* was!

2.) This book in your hands is a testimony to the truth that the Creator Father has your well-being at heart! Re-read, slowly – and meditatively, the pages in this chapter.

3.) Reach for a pencil or a blue pen; take notes. Underline paragraphs. Write your own reflections alongside as you read. Make it your *very* own book!

4.) Most of all, put into practice what you have read. You will soon start noticing dramatic improvements in your friendships and relationships.

5.) If your friends ask: *"Who taught you to dramatically change in your dealings with me as to make me desire a deeper level of relationship with you?"*; willingly share this book with them! Better still, just place a gift order copy of same as a token of your appreciation of God's gift upon my life! Without appearing to make a merchandise of you, these messages on these pages will revolutionize their lives, too!

6.) Lastly, let *my* Friend, Jesus Christ be your friend, too!

En route a Wholesome Friendship

At the end of each of the preceding chapters, I have offered you – by way of suggestion – additional resource-list(s) that I trust would enrich you. Let me proceed a step further, extending unto you my very right hand of friendship.

Allow me to become *your* coach, mentor – and unsurprisingly, *your* friend! Whether – or otherwise – you decided to make Jesus Christ the Lord and Savior of your life, write me today; I'd love to read from you.

Those who desire that I pray with them – or mail them some literature that will enable them to grow in their walk with the Savior, should please also write in!

If you live in a city where *The Harvestways Int'l Church* is located, I'd be more than glad to introduce to you, our able shepherds. Make contact with me today; quality wholesome friendships await you, just a "click" away:

Visit our website: www.harvestways.org
Write an email: reverendsammy@harvestways.org
Join me on Facebook: "Sammy O Joseph"
Tweet me on Twitter: SammyOJoseph

On the ground, send your mail to:
Sammy Joseph Ministries,
Box 15129, Birmingham, England, B45 5DJ.
Telephone: (+44) 7854675159

When we connect, please do *not* forget to include your name, country of origin, address and telephone information with which I may be able to return your kind gesture!

Thank you for demonstrating your trust in my integrity – and in *Sammy Joseph Ministries.*

As the title suggests, *'Sex and Sexuality in Committed Relationships'* is essentially intended for married couples – as well as anyone involved in a serious relationship with the opposite sex. It does not contain graphic language – and may be deemed suitable for anyone who is eighteen years or older!

"Let thy fountain be blessed: and rejoice with the wife of thy youth ...

Let her breasts satisfy thee at all times; and be thou ravished always with her love."

Proverbs 5: 18-19

Chapter 4

Sex and Sexuality in Committed Relationships

"A bundle of myrrh is my wellbeloved unto me; he shall lie all night betwixt my breasts."
Song of Solomon 1:13

Within the preceding pages of this book thus far, I have attempted to help discover *you*. This is because *self-discovery precedes self-identity*. Never in history, has there been such great confusion regarding the identity of self as there currently exists – particularly in the area of human sexuality! When you're at a loss regarding your *true* personality, you will equally be at a loss regarding proper self-actualization and evaluation!

In short, lack of constraints in the physical, moral and sexual departments of *your* life indelibly casts a long shadow upon *your* spiritual *I.D!* This reflection in turn bears exact replicas on *your* physical, daily existence!

Simply put, your physical semblance is a true reflection of your spiritual embodiment – of which sex and sexuality play an intrinsic part!

Your parents, guardians and spiritual overseers may have patronized, placated and cushioned your conscience – having fully complied with the *spirit of religion*; but I beg to differ! My duty is to awaken you to your spiritual and moral obligations. *They* may have been cowardly to *not* have informed you of the truth surrounding your sexuality; but I shall declare unto you what *they* remised. They possibly never informed you that *your* sexuality had been paramount in the mind of the Creator Father, from the *very* beginning. This was an essential reason He had created sex for *your* pleasure – given its usage within the proper context!

A Family, Re-defined

The traditional family setting consists of two parents raising their children. These days however, we have single-parent families. By every means, they are also "families".

Essentially, therefore, a family is a basic social unit of the society related by blood!

If you are a Jesus Christ-follower, then you also have become an essential part of that great big family of God! Therefore, we *not* only have physical families, but also spiritual families!

One essential character common to families – whether physical or spiritual – is their uncommon bonding to common interests and goals. Families primarily share one another's responsibilities. In that wise, family members are *essentially* one another's *homework pieces* that cannot be transferred to *any* third party!

Bring it down to simplicity, the issue of sex, sexuality and the traumatic consequences its misuse continues to cause, *must* be addressed at the very basic grassroots-level of life – that is ideally; in balanced, family-unit settings!

Parents must now lower the hitherto high expectations they have always possessed of the secular classroom teachers to disseminate a wholesome sex education to a group of wild, hormonal fourteen to sixteen year old's, in a once weekly, one-hour long, *Physical and Social Health Education* (*P.S.H.E*) class. Neither can the hour-long, weekly 'Sunday-school' teacher be expected to perform feats of wonders to a youth whose parents have lost both touch and bearing with him/her on issues of sex and sexuality!

Therefore, *every* parent/guardian, I say, *must* prepare to take the bull by its horns: displaying exemplary character-traits before their children/wards, laying them solid moral examples of proper restraints and carefulness in their choices leading fulfilled sex lives and sexuality. *This is the panacea to long lasting emotional traumas in our children!*

The Depravity of our Culture

This fact ought to startle you if your child attends a state-run school: by the time the recess bell had rang, his/her ears would have caught at least four inappropriate swear words or rude innuendos!

Now, that's a very mind-boggling issue for an innocent school-aged child who fails to participate in his/her colleagues' foul-mouthed smut game. More alarming it is when such a *"clean-mouth"* soon becomes a victim of indescribable peer-pressure, alienation, bullying and mean taunts!

This is just a part of *our* culture, the culture we glorify; the culture that daily unveils shocking, sickening revelations of depravity via the media and the music industry – depositing such garbage onto the naïve minds of our children, which in turns spills out in schools' playground conversations!

You probably had watched the talk-show host Oprah Winfrey's interview with Mo'Nique's older brother, Gerald Imes that had claimed screaming world headlines in 2010. In that interview, Gerald Imes publicly – for the very first time – admitted that he had molested his sister Mo'Nique since she was a child of about seven years old. In addition, Mr. Imes admitted the gross sexual abuse had lasted several years.

In a quick twist of tales however, he had also revealed that he himself had been a victim of sexual abuse – and had engaged in the use of drugs since a very tender age! He had been arrested later and sent to prison after having being convicted of abusing another child!

In a related on-line article/commentary in the magazine called *Essence* titled *"Always Listen to Your Kids"* by Gaetane F. Borders, the writer wrote:

> *"Mo'Nique's personal story garnered a lot of Press because of her celebrity. However, her story is a very common one. In fact, one in four girls report being sexually molested before the age of eighteen, and one in six boys report the same.*

> *Therefore, the reality is that at least 25% of you who are reading this article have been sexually abused. Another reality is that only a small percentage of you disclosed this to your parents."*[1]

What's so Wrong with Sex, Afterall?

There is nothing wrong with sex for it to be tagged its taboo status; a banned topic in most parent-teenager, minister-laity forums.

Three Adversarial G's the Puritans – the earlier settlers in America who had sought a holier, purer lifestyle – had been mindful of; they had warned others to be wary of *vainglory, vain pursuits to acquire vain gold,* and *immoral sexual gratification.* If you steered clear of these, they said, your life would be much more meaningful! They couldn't have been be more correct; various parts of the Word of God clearly admonishes same!

Be warned, the desires and cravings to satisfy the lust of the flesh would *not* leave your destiny untarnished. Attempting to feed your soulish desires on sensualistic, egotistic and materialistic tendencies will leave you destitute!

Men and women of pursuit of the *high calling,* from time immemorial, had practiced holiness because the Holy Father God desired it of them. You *could* be holy because He created *your* spirit holy. He commands: *"Be ye holy, for I am holy."*[2]

Then, if a holy God demands that His children live and practise a life of holiness, could there be anything wrong with having sex?

Sex, as the Father heart of God conceived of it, contrary to your thought, is actually holy! It is holy *if* practiced within the confines of a holy matrimony. It is God's perfect gift *to* humans intended for their use within healthy boundaries.

There is therefore, nothing wrong with sex consummated with a legally married spouse; this was the original context within which our fun-loving Creator Father God had purposed it.

Let me share with you, in the next few paragraphs, the reasons why the Creator God added sex and sexuality to the menu of His vast creation.

God's Intent of Sex and Boundaries Within its Usage

• *For married couples only:*
Scripture teaches that Father God intended sex be used *solely* within the confines of a holy matrimony. *Period!* That excludes the use of sex and sexuality in husband/wife-swopping, partnership between un-married cohabitees, civil partnerships between gays, lesbians, bi-curious, trans-gendered, curious and excited teenagers experimenting with foreplay, oral sex – and/or actual penetration.[3]

Father God instituted the marriage covenant. Strategically, He positioned sex as the icing on cake. Lovely sex between a husband and wife is God's gifted invention to the married. Marital sex is holy, desirable, lovely, meaningful and fulfilling!

• *Concerning matured virgins:*

"What of the virgins and singles who are now getting old – and past their years? Are you suggesting they stay calm and composed, preserving their sexuality until they die?"

I perceive your thoughts and fears. So does the heavenly Father! Scriptures admonishes matured virgins and the unmarried past their flower remain strong in *the* faith while learning to *contain* or *"possess their vessels in sanctification and honour."* They are expected of the Father to continue celebrating their singleness, just as their bodies remain productive vessels unto the Lord, even as Dr. Paul wrote in *1 Corinthians 7* – and some other of his epistles. This demand of the Father requires that matured singles possess an undeniable availability of God's grace, particularly, as applicable to *their* sexuality!

Notice, Father God does not expect unmarried singles to live in denial of the fact that they have unfulfilled sexual needs. Rather, He requests of them a faithful, total surrendering of such desires over to the Holy Spirit while drawing daily encouragement, strength and renewal from Him, by faith – and positive interactions with others who are victoriously living the chaste, single, Christian life!

From God's perspective, an unmarried person must desist from casual sex, sex with different multiple partners, sex outside of marriage, "one-night stand's", orgies, etcetera. He/she is expected by the *Father of love* to remain productively single – fully focused, engaged in activities that please the Lord! This is the secret pass-code to conquering discouragement, loneliness, regrets and the clouts of self-pity!

If they have missed the mark – at any point in time on their journey mastering *acceptable* bachelorhood, spinsterhood – or singlehood, they are *not* to remain overcast and downcast by self-pity. They must realize they are on an onward journey unto victory already availed them by the Father heart of God's grace and cleansing power!

• *What do married couples do with sex?*

Married couples engage in sex as a continued renewal and expression of their avowed love and commitment to each other. They celebrate their 'oneness' mainly, through this God-ordained route. Married couples *use* sex to sanctify the sacredness of their celebration of loves! Since this is the case, I envision the face of the Father replete with pleasing smiles and deep satisfaction, whenever He beholds from His Throne, a married couple ooze energy and make uncontrollable moans of ecstasy and delight in each other's arms, consummating their love unto orgasm. (If you lack knowledge but desire to know how to both patiently and lovingly take your wife through the pleasures of attaining an orgasm, I would recommend that you visit your G.P., Pastor – or indeed a local Christian bookshop. Bereft of any shame, order specific literature that addresses your need. I do apologize that it is *not* my intent to diverge away from my original message!)

Sex is not just physical or emotive; rather, the larger part of it is indeed spiritual!

Because emotional and spiritual bonds are created

anytime the sex act is performed, sex therefore, is the covenant that solidifies the bonding of *any* two people engaged in it – regardless of the presence of rubber sheaths of protection! The sex act binds and fuses two spirit-beings, entwining them into just one! This is *the* mysterious sacredness about sex! Therefore, *any* married partner engaging in either an emotional affair or actual sex apart from their wedded spouse commits adultery!

If an unmarried person engages sex with a married one, the unmarried is guilty of fornication! Fornication, adultery or an emotional affair is of grave concern to God and every participant; this issue of sharing spiritual, emotional, psychological and physical members with a stark, bloody stranger! Adultery is the grand betrayal of yourselves, the guilty parties – and not just you, but the innocent one cheated upon! Both adultery and fornication are a grand betrayal against your bodies, souls and spirit!

The betrayal caused by adultery, fornication, sexual sins – and perversions generally, bring brokenness upon *a* body. This brokenness often spills onto *everything* that dwells under the roofs of the perpetrators against *the* marriage covenant, whether it is (adultery) or "bodily covenant" (fornication). Please endeavor to read *1 Corinthians 6:18.*

Sexual sins birth 'pollutions in the land'; they grant an unhindered opening of doors unto devilish and demonic activities, on a great magnitude!

- ### Is sex only for procreation?
The answer to the question above is: *No;* in fact, an

emphatic '*NO!*'

Sex was *not* designed by the Designer Father God *just* for making babies alone. You can relate with your spouse, ravishing her love as King Solomon described in his masterpieces of literature – provided you have *her* consent! I am aware that the issue of "consent" in marriage, granted by the female, is strange to most ears of the inhabitants of the sub-tropical *10/40 window* where the male is perceived as the lion-head of the pride!

However, once a couple has agreed to *coitus*, their circuitry nerve endings commence blinking, extra accurately! *Would you know why?* It is none other reason than the fact that *sex* is on the menu!

When sex is on the menu, anyone meticulously given to details would notice involuntary reflex reactions in the *menu-partakers*! Such reactions in the female as extraordinary warm and bright congenial smiles, an enrichment of the coloration of the eyes, twinkling sparkles in her iris and some excitable quavering in the tone and voice-pitch. If she were in the company of her female counterparts, amidst lady-chats and gossips, you would notice a few 'senseless' giggles when she talks about her agenda for the rest of the day; particularly, her expected triumphant '*conquest*' or '*home-roast*'!

In the male, you would notice an air of extra confident ooze; a deepening of the vocal cords, a spring in his steps; wide, relaxed smiles, a firm grip of the hand during handshakes – and some quite boastful utterances about his wife, to other men, if he also were engaged in "men's talk" with his colleagues!

Most times when two individuals who are deeply *'in love'* have come within close proximities, sexual chemicals released into their blood stream make their bodies surge in an almost unstoppable desire for each other. In such a passionate moment, an unscheduled romp may result. The partner with the higher surge may suddenly switch gears to "overdrive." Talking about *overdrive*, I presume there's something more wholesome to be desired by men *if* – for instance, a godly wife on an enjoyable quiet ride in the country reaches for a caress of her man's hairy hand, gently whispers into his ear: *"Honey, pull the car over, right here; right now! Or take me home – and get me sorted, quickly!"*

Some men are *not* so 'dastardly' in their expressions; so they act in pretense, suppressing the fact that they actually would prefer their wives to be the *racehorse jockey*, rather than they! A few other men get irritated if they needed sex from their wives, but couldn't get it. Some may get frustrated, angry – or become outright aggressive and nasty!

A larger proportion of husbands than you would believe disapproves being labeled as "nasty, irritable, demanding or aggressive" if they forthrightly demand sex from their wives, more often than they are expected to do! This truth will surprise you if you're a wife still inhabiting the land of 'naivety': *any* man in his virile days is ready to make love to the woman he loves for *as many times as she would let him!* This is one reason a wife ought to be sensitive, accommodating her husband's needs, *at all times* with a willing kindness and understanding!

Whatever sexual conclusion the mates reach about meeting their sexual needs; if they are very passionate *not* desirous of making a baby, they should ensure the use of a form of protection or contraception!

Perhaps you are a non-hairy dude with no car in a megacity, screaming: *"Don't hand over the power of a 'sex-jump' over to the female: my wife is sanctimonious! She would never demand for sex, rather she would complain of migraine 90% of times we'd agreed to have sex!"* Well, I have some news for you, both!

Misconceptions about Sex

I would only discuss two major misconceptions that may make a partner withdraw from sex; vis-à-vis:

i.)   Complaints about migraine, and;

ii.) Size-matters!

• *Migraine-complaining couple:*

If this sub-heading caption summarizes you, kindly permit me to make a rich and precious stone deposit into both your joint-account. Here it is: *you must realize that both men and women are "wired" significantly differently in their physique and emotionality. These differences in 'set-up' are as a result of the Creator-Father's default programing!*

The female-male contrasts become even more pronounced as we approach the domains of sex and sexuality. Casting my mind back on memory lane, passage rites were more readily availed me whenever I had done chores around the house. Chores like dutifully changing our toddlers' diapers/ pampers, dishwashing, lawn mowing, gardening and placing the garbage out for the Waste Disposal guys, *etcetera!* At that time in our marriage, I never understood what my serviceability translated into, in my wife's sexuality!

Possibly, you too are at a loss, understanding the feminine translation of sexuality. Well, you're not alone! Let me attempt to intermediate! Hear me clearly, on this major concept: *sex and sexuality in a larger percentage of wives began the moment their husbands began putting actions behind their words!*

It's as simple as that; believe you me!

We know that demonstrative love communicates. It communicates fulfilling visible, productive, 'helpmate' activities/chores and appropriate actions/re-actions; not just empty words that have proven over time to be ordinary sweet talk!

'That could be a hasty generalization', you opine! However, I reassure you would fair well to agree with my position on demonstrative love!

Not only must your words communicate visible, productive actions to your wife, her relationship menu specifically tailored to her taste ought to send you on a pathway of discovery – discovering her femininity and personality!

An honorable man sets time apart, therefore, to discover what love language his spouse speaks and thereafter, learns to speak the same. If he does, I most assuredly can affirm that *their* sex lives, both, will be greatly enhanced - and fulfilled.

Enduring sharp, migraine thumps in the head is a real menace to any sufferer. Migraine must *not* be sidelined or neglected; it is *not* different to any other disease.

As such, it must be addressed the same way as other diseases are addressed, using the name of JESUS!

Any child of the heavenly Father, experiencing a *dis*-ease must appropriate the full-payment already accredited their *health-account* by those many stripes that had lacerated the body of the Lord Jesus, the Anointed One of the Father! *This is a crucial piece of liberating truth the sick, ill, "dis"-eased, distressed or poverty-stricken must appropriate to their menacing situations.*

Hear this "word of wisdom": if you experience migraine at scheduled sex time(s) when you ought to be maximizing and harnessing "togetherness" with your husband, please kindly inquire from families *if any* progenitors or distant relatives ever felt same – at such times. If your sampling polled positive, that surely must be taken as an indication that your blood-lineage could have been suppressed under *a* specific ancestral or generational curse, for so long!

What could you do?

You would appropriate same blood and the stripes of the Lord Jesus Christ, to ensure and effect your deliverance, requesting the help of your *priest*, your husband! As your priest, the man "over you" is authorized of God, to destroy this gripping power of *the* thief, which has interfered with and stolen the maximizing of your sexuality away from you! All you would need do is stand in agreement with him as he effects your rescue! Notice, when you pray agreeing with your spouse, you are *not* doing anything different to just cashing in on the check that had been deposited into your health account by your loving Heavenly Father! (You both do this same thing if the devil is tormenting *any* other area(s) of your lives – and/or those of your children).

More couples ought to learn that good, slow, prolonged romance, followed by exquisite lovemaking surely does relieve built-up pressure within their bodies, thus opening up more capillaries for increased blood flow.

A good sex session therefore, causes the release of "feel-good", relaxation-inducing, stress-relieving chemical hormones – such as *endorphin* – into the bloodstream! Similarly, *oxytocin*, which helps induce relaxation, reduce high blood pressure and high cortisol level is also released during a pleasurable sex session! This chemical intrinsically possesses natural pain-relieving powers!

Because of these facts, instead of becoming a pain-reliever-self-prescribing-wife, you ought to reach for *the* pain-killer: *your* husband! Gently reach out to him at such "migraine feeling" times; mold your curves round his "bulges" – and entwine your arms in each other's, in a loving tango!

Teach him, communicating with him how best to "serve" you! Open up your entire beings unto each other – fondling, nibbling, kissing, making love *very* gently and passionately.

- ### *Size-matters:*
Another misconception for *not* having sex is a naïve spouse's excuse that their partner's excess body weight

– whether male or female – and/or 'manhood' size or small vaginal entry would constitute an inhibiting factor to an enjoyable sex. This supposition only reveals to an understanding mind, an inkling of mediocrity!

Arguably, there could be some other un-revealed, underlying issues begging for a revelation, here! Possibly, you desire of him/her to lose weight – but wouldn't know how best to approach the subject. Each time you brought it up in a loving discussion, it always met stiff opposition. Maybe his enriched endowment causes you pain when he *impatiently* enters or *selfishly* clasps you, in the passions of a 'meet' – and whenever you tried to bring it to his attention, he always turned up open-palms!

Whatever your situation, kindly permit me to offer you some help, both!

Candidly speaking, an excess body weight, a small vaginal orifice or a huge manhood size *alone* should *not* continue to cause you to possess tainted memories of pleasures or induced feelings of being "used". There are *a hundred and one* ways to ravish your love without inducing any residual pain physically, mentally, genitally or emotionally. There is a workable knowledge of the workings of both a woman's and a man's body you *must* possess. There is a *"how to"*; to bypassing your fears and inhibitions.

Perhaps, a visit to the gynecologist is all that is needed. You may in addition approach a nice Christian bookstore and purchase some nice christian counseling books and DVD's that teach about the *"how to's"* of the topic in *situ*! Share these rich resources with each other, unashamedly

– and practice what enriching information you've gained! Greatly enhance the crucial sex and sexuality departments of your marriage unto victory. I have listed some book resources on the last page of this chapter, that I believe should be of help to you!

Marital sex is a blessing in many ways than could be conceived. Reports from published counseling authors reveal that married couples who have sex regularly stay fitter, healthier and live longer fulfilled lives of productivity. From Ministers of Religion unto Pastors, Medical Doctors (G.P's), Judges, Lawyers and Barristers unto Politicians, Public speakers, Airplane pilots and Flight attendants; these professionals, who have *been well served* by their spouses have always demonstrated an additional noticeable anointing for productivity. They usually have delivered with twinkles in their eyes and merry-filled hearts. Since their *cups* are emotionally and sexually full, they are neither distractible nor thirsty to drink from another's brook! Their lifestyles, ministries, vocations and offices are exemplary and blameless!

Why shouldn't yours be, too?

Snapshot of a Man's Sexuality Compared with a Woman's

"I made a covenant with mine eyes: why then should I think upon a maid?"

Job 31:1

Job was a very godly successful Jewish farmer and business-executive. His question, quoted above, is an apt description of the generality of men; irrespective of geographical location, color, race or creed. According to Job's observation, *just* an innocuous thought of a beautiful woman upon the male's mind *should be deemed* as sufficient enough to fan into flames, his engorged appetites – if he has *not* learned to contain his *male-ness.*

Six thousand years after Job's precise warning, the greatest Rabbi that ever lived, added the element of looking at – or viewing derogatorily – a woman, as fully qualified as the very act of adultery, itself. His exact words?

> *"But I say unto you that everyone who so much as looks at a woman with evil desire for her has already committed adultery with her in his heart."*
> Matthew 5:28; Amplified Version.

In other words, a mere picture, stored mental imagery or a memory flashback of the female anatomic/exterior features in an un-regenerated male's mind – or that of a lad lacking basic *sight-discipline* could induce an arousal within him! Some naïve women still find this truth very strangely incomprehensible!

If that weren't true, why should there still exist striptease, lap-dancing/gents' clubs and escort services?

Thence, real *husband-keepers* know this secret; that to keep the fire of sexuality passionately glowing in the hearts of their husbands is essentially, *the* major way to *keep* them, eternally! Serving delicious meals of venison *may* occupy a backburner place, to sex, in his mind!

Sex and hot delicious meals on time are great; however, in an almost equal token, wives *must* endeavor to continually keep themselves both pleasurable and desirable in the eyes of their husbands much, as the fruit in the Garden of Eden had been *"pleasant to the eyes"* of mother Eve.[6]

Succinctly explained therefore, a wife ought not to disengage with the processes that ensure her entire being is irresistibly desirable and sumptuously pleasing to her husband — long past their wedding day and a passion-filled honeymoon!

Permit God's Holy Spirit to illuminate your mind as you ponder upon these questions:

- *Why would soiled, odious, menstrual pads/tampons be carelessly dumped in a corner of your marital bedroom? The truth does not excuse used pads and tampons being hygienically disposed off, the moment they come off-duty!*

- *Why wouldn't a woman desire to wash herself, at least, daily?*

- *Why would any husband desire to attempt to kiss a wife who has refused to learn to brush her teeth and tongue, dental floss and gargle?*

- *What's so appealing in a vindictive wife who decides to either keep malice, indulge in a reckless spending-spree and/or nag her husband anytime she feels 'low' or offended?*

- *If her husband is inclined towards education, learning and skills-enhancements — and has been requesting his wife to advance and enhance her skills in her chosen field of interest over the months, why would she decline and rather prefer to rest on her oars of just a Baccalaureate, G.E.D, G.C.S.E or even a first degree; for instance, in the 21ˢᵗ century?*

Any woman who desires that her relationship with her partner thrives ought to understand how an un-disciplined, ill-disciplined *"Johnny"* could so easily be steered straight into the arms of some silly "sweet plums" – just because those *fruits* fulfilled the basic law of attractiveness; being ordinarily *pleasant to the eyes!*

So if you've been wondering, *"Why would 'Johnny' ever leave me, despite all these years of togetherness?";* well, that's exactly what I've been trying to explain to you! *Silly 'Johnny' decided he's had enough of you because you've become myopic, obstinate – and have refused to re-invent yourself as to be both relevant in an ever-changing world, pleasant and desirable to his eyes – and possibly, his ears!*

To such displeased *"Johnny's"*, would you realize that righteous Job's name is forever etched in fire, onto the golden scroll of Heaven's Hall of Fame?[7]

Would you bother to love to know how that became possible?

Mr. Job had got his name onto God's pen's tip because while he'd lived on earth, he *had* strictly *"made a covenant with his eyes"* to *not* wander and ponder with lust upon a female, that was *not* his avowed wife! His example secured the chances of many other men's names being indelibly fire-etched into Father God's golden scroll.

So could yours, too!

Not only do men differ significantly from women in the way their eyes communicate with their minds, their minds with their emotions, their emotions with their groins (*if* they visualize eroticism or embed a female's posture on their minds); *the male specie does indeed experience a pressure-build-up in his groins/scrotal area, for the production of sperm – the male reproductive seed!*

As this pressure reaches "saturation" level, his body "switches on" its mechanisms to capably rid excess sperm, naturally – through either his urine or a surprising "wet dream".

Any abstaining male, regardless of age, status, ethnicity or culture, may encounter "wet dreams!" Similarly, a married man who has *not* had a sexual encounter with his wife "for a while" could find himself suddenly 'plagued' by "wet dreams" – as could be the situation where:

- *either of the spouses is suffering from life-threatening illness(es),*

- *either a couple is separated due to work-demands across states and borders; or,*

- *the couple are legally separated – or divorced!*

If you happen to fit into any of these descriptions, above – and therefore experience a "wet dream", please do *not* induce any self-guilt! Neither is there any cause for a medical alarm! The Creator Father God had you and your sexuality, in mind before the onset of your creation!

Closely easily confused or associated with "wet-dreams" is the masturbation practice, which I shall be discussing sooner than later, in the next few pages. But for now, let's look at a woman's sexuality!

Snapshot of a Woman's Sexuality Compared with a Man's

A woman's views of sexuality – and what is "pleasant to *her* eyes"; that is, sexually appetizing to *her* – are entirely different to a man's. Additionally, sexual tastes, desires and energy vary from one woman to another!

Primarily, a woman's sexual fulfillment is somewhat connected to her emotional fulfillment – via a link conjoined with every other going-on's in her life. A wife who witnesses the commitment and support her husband invests leading his home spiritually, helping advance her career and ministry (if she is the career/ministry-type) and providing for her and their children – if there are any, will perennially *dwell in love* with her husband.

Other positive activities from a dutiful husband that will keep his wife's emotional measure perked up to the brim include: his commitment and dutifulness towards *her* family; his serviceability and availability. More, his helping to walk the dog(s), feed the pets; lawn mow, unblock drainages, do 'helpful' chores around the house, take pivotal roles in paying the bills and looking after her general interests will automatically make a wife feel loved – and *secure! (If he can swat flies, rid the house of spiders and mice – those should be added bonuses!)*

For a husband to act contrariwise to his avouched wife would be synonymous to a firefly flirting with open flames!

This is the point I am trying to establish: "Husband, the more interconnected you are with the intricacies of your wife's life, the more attractive, desirable and irresistible you will become in *her* eyes." In other words, the more you serve *her* interests, just as Christ serves His Church's, the more sexually-desirable you would become to her. Similarly, the more disposed she would become towards you, generally, drawing closer to you with her entire spirit, soul and body – opening unto you as the floral petals do, the sun's rays!

Why? Because her heart firmly trusts in the stability of *your* love!

Herein lies the mystery shrouded in femininity: once a woman's heart can truly vouch for her husband's true love, she's eternally his, without compromise!

Similarly, most women will be surprised to learn that a significant majority of men still do *not* understand how a woman's emotions can be influenced by periodical changes in her body! *The* truth is that a woman's sexual desire does indeed revolve around that period in her life, when her hormonal secretions "yell out" loudest, their greatest reproductive potency and availability.

- *Oh, girl; did you think he understood, for instance, that much of your menstrual cycle is inconvenient?*

- *Sir, did you not know that some females still are not well acquainted with their bodies, feelings, emotions and desires – and could dwell in a haze of internalized, unspoken confusion in the sub-consciousness, for a long while?*

Isn't this the essence of her need for your often re-assurances?

- *Man, didn't you know that you stifled her self-confidence when, instead of re-assurances, you began comparing her with her friend Jill, "Johnny's" wife or a Hollywood personality?*

Are you following my thread of thoughts, sir?

Some days, your woman feels very tender and ready to receive you; yet on a not-so-good-day, she would be willing to snarl at you like a Rottweiler, should you venture near her, in your usual, predictive, crude manner! Certainly, those are *not* the times to sing *The Archies' "Hey Sugar, Ho Honey, Honey, You're my Candy girl!"* in her periphery! If you loved *you*, you would retreat or back-off, once she dismisses *you* with a hand wave of a disinterest!

Now, do you suppose that a sensible lady would *fall* for – let alone marry a thug? If she said, "I do" to you; you must have meant everything to her. Now, if that was the case '*Why would you berate her intelligence by letting-go of yourself and suddenly cultivating a habit of laziness and an unwillingness to work and earn a living, fourteen years down the marriage-lane just because you were laid off work, seven months ago?*'

You may be able rationalize your demeaning state of being to yourself – but whatever has turned you "lazy" certainly would *not* in the very least be "pleasant to your wife's eyes".

Listen, a man is expected to *man up* to his *manhood!* The Creator-Father designed men with square shoulders to work, earn a living and provide for their families. Shake off mediocrity therefore and rather voraciously hunt for a means of living before you approach her with the issue of sex.

I quite understand gender role-plays in our modern world, where, sometimes, the wife wears the trouser while the husband minds the home and tends the children. Sure, there is nothing wrong with your style, if both couple have a great understanding, respect and love for each other – knowing fully well that they are both a team! In such special cases, in-laws and friends must be made to understand their choice of preference, running their home and marriage. No slight should be welcomed from any quarter regarding their re-arrangements.

Just like I did ask the female earlier, then permit God's Holy Spirit to illuminate your mind, too, as you ponder upon *your* responses to these questions:

- *When you dated your wife, you did everything to win her approval. Most of all, you listened to her emotions – and empathized with her! Why would you now disregard, ignore and continue making no time available to listen to her anymore, other than when you desire sex?*

This is why she *feels* emotionally abused and used! This explains her inconsolable weeping and tears. *You* – unbeknown to you – are "killing her emotions", softly.

Do you get it, "Johnny"?

- *Why would you dishonor her by not seeking her advice in decision-making?*

- *To what purpose would your heavily soiled pair of socks be serving, when carelessly dumped on her blouse in the washing*

124

basket; such socks with such a choking stench that pervades the entire house?

This is plain, stark disregard for *her* – you may call it what else suits you!

• *If you indeed love her as you profess to do, "Why wouldn't you desire to wash yourself, at least, daily – and each time, before sex?" If you're a foreman who has been busy all day at work, what prohibits you from soaking yourself in an evening warm bath before bedtime?*

• *Why should a wife desire to kiss a husband bereft of maintaining the very 'basics' of an hygienic lifestyle: teeth brushing, tongue-washing, dental flossing and gargling?*

• *What's so appealing in a bully of a man whose emotions are so warped that he resorts to mind-control games – or becomes a scrooge who denies others' happiness by every means, once he's experienced a hurt or disappointment?*

• *Why wouldn't a husband cultivate the art of romancing his wife? It is not virtuous to give a lame excuse such as "I am not the romantic type" as the many men who wrongly under estimate their capabilities and potentials have always done.*

If you're bereft of excuses, therefore, try this today: be honest as you ask your heart-throb: *"Will you teach me to be romantic? What can I do better – and how should I set about it?"* Asking her such a question itself is the beginning of cultivating the art of romance!

The negating of these – and more, are *the* reasons *some*

married women delve into affairs, or disavow their professed first love.

I hope both of you will work at your relationship and make yours, affair-proof!

Sexual Libido & Masturbation

You may be disabled or carrying an 'at-risk pregnancy'. You may have recently lost a loved one – and become a widow/widower. Your spouse may have requested from you, a period of separation, so that you both could work at your marriage that it results not in divorce. You may be divorced – or indeed, just a long-time single person! Could it be that you work far away from home, and could only meet your spouse, a weekend fortnightly?

Whatever your circumstance, irrespective of your gender, I may safely predict that there comes moments in *your* sexuality when your libido hits the roof! At such times – depending on factors such as youthfulness, health and vigor; you *will* strongly, intensely desire to have sex!

Given a prominent, sufficient level of testosterone in a male's blood stream – coupled with the natural 'build-up' of sperm over time, as earlier explained; a male *will* naturally feel inclined to desire sex! (Testosterone is that chemical component which when released into the blood, defines *maleness* and male-characteristics. Traces of testosterone secretion, however, have been found present in some females, too!)

The female libido pushes for the same sex drive as in men: ensuring she desires to touch or be touched, cuddle or be cuddled – and 'very specially loved'!

Some women at such times of libido-peak discover an uncanny craving for chocolates; others, for a good lick of an iced-cream! A few other females, still, would choose a horse-ride over a furious bicycle ride on a bumpy, 'earthy' country road! Yet, a quieter female may just desire a cuddly-feel with her teddy!

Unlike in males, the female libido is insidious, 'hidden', non-intrusive and most often, non-aggressive. However, it could still be very profoundly overwhelming in some females! If at those special moments when her sexual desire peaks, there arises within her, a longing thought *for* her husband or lover, a woman could be 'set in motion' for days, on end. *This is very much unlike her male counterpart!*

Sexual drives vary from person to person. Sexual libido, certainly, is a healthy component of the Creator God's design in the sex and sexuality functions of humans. Therefore, it is wholesome and purely delightsome. Sexual libido certainly is *not* demonic – that is, *not* from Satan.

Now, when this natural 'hunger' bites, what would you do?

I possibly overheard a female whisper: *'It would be time for bunnies 'n batteries!'* And a male: *'Just an appropriate time to approach the self-help desk!'* Both expressions translate to just one word: *'masturbation'.*

Indeed, masturbation has existed with humans, as early

as the very dawn of discovery. It is one of the keenly contested areas of discussion in religion, morality and ethics. The governmental departments of health and education, churches and ministries, parents and couples approach it's discussion from differing perspectives. *One truth I most assuredly declare of the Lord unto you is that there is never a reference in the holy writ where masturbation was mentioned, commended or condemned.* Neither does masturbation drive anyone insane – or there would have been more insane people, today, in our society more than there currently are!

Additionally, masturbation certainly does *not* increase the level of promiscuity in teenagers: *anyone* desperate to tow a line of depravity needed no guidance in this age of "one-touch" social interconnectivity. Thus, I believe, that religiously indoctrinated parents and spouses ought to update their understanding on this topic before inducing guilt onto the consciences of their adolescents – and possibly, partners.

Notes of Caution on Masturbation

Note carefully these cautionary notes on the act of masturbation:

i.) *Masturbation can become addictive:*

Masturbation can become addictive – and thus short-circuit the very essence of intimacy the Father-Creator of pleasures intended for, in a married couple, consummating their 'loves'.

ii.) *Masturbation may place the 'practitioner' in a dire danger of becoming addicted to self-gratification:*

Essentially, only a minority few indulge in masturbation practice yet escape becoming addicted to self-pleasure. Rather, *many* become so engrossed with selfishly pleasing themselves that they completely neglect, ignore, alienate, not *long* for, or completely *not* desire their spouse in sexual relations. This could become a potentially dangerous situation in *any* marriage.

iii.) *Masturbation can be fueled by a fantasy which borders on lust:*

An imagination of another's imagery in the mental, emotional, or soulish realms whilst engaging in sex with a spouse is essentially lustful! Such fantasizing will erode and weaken – until it breaks – the *very* bonds of unity of such marriages!

I had counseled a couple many years ago; the husband would turn to the wall close to the bed, after a disagreement with his wife. Later in the evening when the wife had crept into bed, willing to make peace with him – and had offered her 'vessel' as 'the appeasing sacrifice', the husband's insensitivity and utter self-gratification had led to further humiliation of the wife. Needless to say, their marriage had ended in a divorce.

iv.) *Danger of depleting energy reserves:*

Masturbation *may* offer a temporary relief to your sexual urge; *not* a lasting solution! This "sexual relief" comes with such price-tags as tiredness, grogginess and the depletion of precious energy reserves which would have been hitherto utilized in the "reasonable service" of God in prayer, personal bible study, going out on witnessing and evangelism – *etcetera!*

Instead of masturbating, you could make a wiser choice to invest your energy reserves in engaging in a refreshing sex with your spouse or mentoring your children in life-coaching lessons as required in energy-demanding outdoor activities such as fishing, boating, running *etcetera*![8]

v.) Aiding/preventing premature ejaculation:
Continuous masturbation by a man battling the emotive, psychological problem of premature ejaculation could ensure his efforts end in a lost battle! Since masturbation centers only upon pleasuring self, further engaging in the act may weaken such a man's abilities to "hold out" longer before reaching a sexual climax, which would have been much more desirable for both he and his wife.

Some medical experts on the other hand suppose that masturbation could help enhance a man's delay of ejaculation – just before he reaches an orgasm; he squeezes the frenulum until an erection subsides!

Having debated the *pros* and *cons* of masturbation, since scriptures are silent on it, I deem it wise also, *not* to take sides on the issue! However, I would presume the following facts, that:

- *You* possess a 'working knowledge' of *your* body – which hasn't been *leased* unto you by Father God either to be abused or misused[9];

- *You* are in touch with *your* sexuality; and,

- The Holy Spirit possesses *you*!

Because of my declared assumptions, I trust – therefore that *you* are at liberty to do as *you* are led!

Becoming a Better Person

"Better individuals make a better community, a better community, a better people, a better people, a better citizenry – and a better citizenry, a better world!"

Sammy Joseph

Better individuals make *any* establishment work – even *better!* So, whether you want to become a better friend, a better spouse, a better husband, a better wife, a better father, a better mother, a better brother, a better sister, or indeed, a better *you*; I have presented in bullet points, proven suggestions that will help you achieve that inner yearning, desire and calling!

Therefore, to become a better person in *any* relationship:

i.) *Communicate clearly with one another, the expectations and goals of your relationship:*
The lack of understanding of and non-clarity about expectations and goals added to the unwillingness to shoulder the *onus of responsibility* of tasks continue to wreck relationships.

Ensure each party understands the *"workable"* expectation-requirements of the relationship. Accept to play *your* part in achieving those goals and expectations. Encourage your partner(s) to do the same.

ii.) *Set healthy, mutually acceptable and practicable boundaries:*
Set healthy, mutually acceptable boundaries – and agree to respect those boundaries.

iii.) Base your relationship on truth, honesty and openness.

iv.) Be real – not surrealistic – in your expectations: Disappointment is the gap of difference between expectation and reality. To lower your disappointment, you must learn to keep your expectations attainable and realistic!

v.) Work hard at your relationships: Every successful venture demands hard work. Don't give up when the 'rough patches' begin to be revealed in your friendships/relationships – because they certainly will! Remember, we *all* possess some rough edges.

vi.) Be appreciative – even of tiniest gestures of kindness.

vii.) Say what you mean and mean what you say!

viii.) Forgive each other, easily: Forgive each other, easily and repeatedly – *not* repeating your spouse's, children's, relative's or friend's faults either to yourself, other friends – or foes. At work, possess tact and loyalty. Be professional! At play, show understanding. Be fair! With blood relations, be calm. Love so unconditionally!

With distant blood relations, be cautious! If the Lord had intentionally included cousin Judas in His team of disciples, there is all likelihood that you may confidently nominate onto your team just one distant blood relative, who may just turn to be a nasty hater! Harness your mind, in advance – and watch your ways!

If you are divorced – and seeking new love, tempted as you may become to spill the beans about your *ex*, always restrain yourself from repeating his/her faults to a potential new person when they arrive your shores. Be willing to demonstrate growth vis-à-vis forgiveness by forgetting the past – and healing up!

ix.) Make allowance(s) for offences to occur in your relationships and don't be upbeat – neither 'beaten up' by them:

There are people who dwell in a state of "mind-readiness", eagerly expecting their friend's/spouse's fatal mistake or error of judgment. This negative state of mind isn't what I prescribed!

Rather, like a tailor/fashion-designer anticipating sewing a new designer wear, you're requested to order additional yards of clothing material than the exact you needed to sew, making *huge allowances* in your tailoring estimation. This is how you harness your mind with that mindset already incorporated with "allowances for others' errors of judgments".

This mindset isn't caught unawares by an offensive, tactical, surprise move! Foresight is another name for this pre-engaged mind-set type!

Switch onto your "eagle-vision" goggles, therefore – *"bearing with one another and making allowances"* for offences, because you love one another.[10]

Becoming a Better Wife

The following are my suggestions to becoming a better wife to your husband:

i.) Establish and maintain the essence of good communication:

At the heart of every communication dwells a deep desire to gain an understanding of what idea lies in the other person's mind. Humans achieve this through dialog!

Talk! Talk!! Talk!!!

Establish and maintain the use of good communication.

Engage the use of lofty words to praise his efforts. Tell him how handsome – and dear to you, he is, using *your own* words. Never assume he already knows.

Preferably, do *not* communicate your displeasure to him with angry looks in your moments of displeasure. Rather, you should *study* to gain an appropriate window of opportunity whereby you may request of him, a discussion/dialog. Any woman who implements this suggestion has demonstrated self-control, tact and respect for her *crown!*

Now, you could be in for a surprise, because this dude – in his quest to compartmentalize life's happenings – may *not* have been mindful at all, of having offended or wronged you! Therefore, a gracious wife *must* refrain from labeling her husband with a ready, handy label of insensitivity – or otherwise, before having first lovingly "confronted" him. Remember, the word *"confrontation"* in the original Latin *"confrontari"* exclusively suggests the idea of *"putting head to head".* Confrontation, therefore, revolves around *"dialog",* much like we see at the United Nations!

Ordinary dialog, communicating by asking a simple question with a soft tongue – *not* in a harsh tone demanding rights, would be of great help. *It will save you a pot of hassles!* Rich communication does *not* have to be complicated. However, it makes a whole world of difference in relationships, generally! *Remember, we share a common ability to communicate, dialog and confront if we choose to!* Men are from neither Mars – nor women, from Venus, after all!

ii.) *Honor, esteem and appreciate your husband:*
Represent your husband honorably and honestly, to everyone you talk about him to, outside of your bedroom walls! You do not need to put up 'cover-up' acts – but you owe him that loyalty to honor, respect and esteem him before your children, families and friends – including neighbors and colleagues!

You probably *cannot* continue to put up with the "tattling and prattling" of friends who dishonor their husbands. Quietly excuse yourself – and exit such 'fellowships'; that is the greatest respect and honor you can award *yourself* and your marriage!

Notice, when we honor spiritual authorities, scripture teaches we are directly honoring the Father God.[11]

iii.) *Respect his viewpoints and counsel on issues bordering on decision-making:*

Endeavor *not* to make "major" decisions without consulting your spouse; it goes either way! Nothing damages a man's ego as a wife who discounts his viability and counsel, proceeds to make a "major" decision, anyway, ir-respective of what he opines. Yet, major decisions in marriage are supposed to be jointly made!

If you have children, you would agree with me the need to include them, at some point, in *some* of your decision-making processes!

You may *not* totally agree with your husband's viewpoint; nevertheless, thank him anyway, for his suggestions and counsel. Let him know you value his counsel – and will be open to moderate your thoughts, *if need be*. This will make him respect your wisdom, uniqueness and individuality – even more!

iv.) *When a husband requests sex from his wife, she should not brush him off like a pest on a pet:*
If a man has *not* been sexually "served" for a while, it is *not* unlikely that it won't be long before he requests it from his wife! (Please, re-read *Snapshot of a Man's Sexuality compared with a Woman's* on page 116).

Presumably, the wife may be ill disposed in body, mind or feelings so that she is unable to engage in sex at the time of his requisition. If this was true, such wife in this predicament should neither presume *nor* assume her husband's pre-knowledge of her "ailment(s)" or ill disposition. She should *not* also view him as a 'sex-pest.' Rather, she ought to appreciate the fact that he's fond of her, in love with her, judging her as "pleasant to his eyes" to request 'a deal' off her! She must radiantly accept his gesture, as fully complimentary!

This wife *should* endeavor, therefore, to show great concern for her spouse, re-assuring him, with such a statement as: *"Let me pulverize this over in my mind first – and I will get back to you, as soon as possible; my promise, love!"* She may then plant a kiss on his forehead! Otherwise, she may readily negotiate to meet him 'halfway' at such inclement seasons – whilst she fully recuperates in order to be able to *fully* acquiesce him. Such loving acts like frolicking, tender kissing, love-feeding, nibbling and 'necking'; skin-to-skin warm embraces, sensual caresses and cuddles are acceptable *smorgasbord* in replacement of a 'full menu'. Her kindness will be highly appreciated by an honorable man of virtue who possesses good understanding!

v.)   Organize surprise events for him:
Organize for your hubby, a *'surprise'* event you alone know he will love! Treat him great! Your 'surprise' event could chart you, both, a course of a long romantic walk, in a quiet field leading to the meadow! Or you could lead him into the woods on a mild day – where you'd impart onto him a love-lesson he'd live to never forget!

Remember, this is *your* thing!

You may surprise him by throwing an honorable birthday party/celebration in his honor – when you know he wasn't keen on celebrating one; or possibly, take him out to *Marks & Spencer* on a spending spree! *(Who says a woman can't lavish money on her man?)*

Possibly, if you can afford it without creating a dent in the family budget, your "surprise" package-plan may include going on a vacation with him only, to a location/ spot you've always known he would be keen on visiting. If you both are an outdoor-type couple, you may opt for jet-skiing, speed-boat racing, kayaking, quad biking, sky-diving, or a romantic swim in the ocean on a sunny day when the tides are not a threat to lives!

You finalize *your* decision! Your *quality motive* organizing a "surprise" in his honor is to reveal to him, your appreciation of him. Your *mundane intent*, of course: feed both your emotions! Remember, the male specie has emotions, too!

vi.) Finally, wife, pray for your husband:
The devil hates "coverings" – whether physical, social, financial or spiritual. *"Coverings" depict hierarchical orderliness.* A marriage, for instance, is Father God's original intent for covering both couple – the husband being the ultimate spiritual "covering" over his wife! The devil, God's archenemy hates this fact; therefore, he fights tooth and nail over healthy marriages that they *not* stand! But yours will stand – grow and thrive, triumphantly!

Successful marital races commence not at *"On your marks!"* but *"On both spouses' knees!"* This is where divine power is availed many healthy strong homes and marriages.

Many battles await a righteous man, but with the support of a praying godly wife, there awaits him resounding victories. This paraphrase renders better my intent:

"Many are the afflictions of a godly husband, but a prayerful wife avails him, mighty deliverances!"

Becoming a Better Husband

The following are my suggestions to becoming a better husband to your wife:

i.) Cultivate the art of effective communication:

Praise your wife always. Your words carry power; therefore sway your power, effectively and positively. Use positive words to build up your wife. Tell her how much you *do* love her! Don't ever say again: *"She knows I love her";* that statement is passive. You must choose to be actively engaged in the use of your words of love.

She needed being told, many times, daily, how much you love her. Desire to fill her emotional tank – to the brim, always!

A healthy man seeks to learn the art of effective communication with the help of his wife. Effective communication requires the dexterous skill of listening, on the part of *most* men. Therefore, endeavor to create a positive atmosphere in your home conducive for great dialog/communication. Be available, so that your wife and children may be able to discuss with you, whenever the need arises.

Be approachable, too, emotionally!

Not every male is reticent of issues that are akin to be addressed. A 'healthy' male is *not* uncommunicative. Lack of communication in the male occurs when his ego has suffered considerable damage; otherwise, every "healthy" male *does* communicate! What is required of a woman of understanding, therefore, is to perfect the art of "drawing out" the king on the inside of him! *He has a king within him; you, the woman of great understanding gently, persuasively lead and usher him out!*

Real men can – and do effectively communicate! They talk "great" about their wives, children, jobs and careers. They boast of visions, aims, aspirations and projects. They are fanatical about their favorite sports and teams – not forgetting their newest *rides* and gadgetry. Men who are doing well, brag about their well doing. Catch a 'real' man on these issues – and he'd probably out-talk you!

Men who bottle their feelings, on the other hand, are probably insecure, immature or wounded spiritually and emotionally. In most single mother-homes where the fathers were never known, but the strictest mothers had raised young males, the emotions of these young men could have become warped or damaged. The reason is simply apparent: a lion's cubs always pride after the majestic way the alpha male leads the pride! Such are the indelible impacts purposeful male figures impart on their young, in our homes! (Now, imagine how many things do go wrong in the absence of an alpha male, marking his territory, in the wild forest!)

It would accost the grace of God – and the special enduring, patience of a godly wife to help nurture unto healing, a married male wounded from childhood turmoil. In high probability, such a male may just keep revolving around the orbits of hurt and bitterness – even as a grown adult! This male, I would advise, *must never*, in his moments of displeasure, communicate with his wife and/children with *his* looks, mouth, hands or legs! *No, sir!*

Any aggrieved angry male must learn to discipline himself to walk, miles ahead of his emotions. This is an essential pre-requisite course in the art of effective communication in wounded males! He *must* first, rigorously equip himself with the discipline of verbalizing his emotions on a piece of paper alone, in a quiet room, in the heat of displeasure! After he'd calmed down enough to handle issues *only* may he return to his spouse/partner to – without the use of any other body member – dialog *"in love."*[2]

A man *must* always remember that though his physique may be sturdy and strong, yet, he's been physically built up, by nature, only to *build up* and *work hard* to nurture his wife, children – and many others whom the good Lord may send across his pathways to access his help! Hence, a 'real' man does *not* physically, emotionally, verbally and/or fiscally violate his wife and/children citing: *"That's the only language she/they understand(s)!"*

Real men do *not* violate anyone, in any way. Real men learn the art of communication – and engage *"communication"* in its effective uses.

ii.) *Approved use of non-verbal communication:*
One approved use of non-verbal communication a godly man gives his spouse is that wink; a twinkling eye and a heart-stirring smile that communicates: *'Go, baby; I am proud of you!'* He should avail her more of such winks. *Nothing so gladdens the heart of a female as a male that could*

141

make her heart, smile!

Flirt indiscriminately with your queen. Flirt with your boyish looks and rippling muscles. If you're blessed to still possess your six-pack abdomen, flaunt it before her, time and again! You will rock *her* world!

Smile, laugh, giggle, look at her from the corner of your eyes; send her *thumbs-up's* that will make her heart melt! Sing her love songs – even if you're not confident you can carry a tune! That makes it even funnier! When you are at dinner – within, or on a date without, – sneak your leg within hers; tug at her calf with your toe. Look deeply into her eyes – and pretend it wasn't you!

From time to time, buy her nice flowers that you know she would love!

These are some effective communication techniques that require no verbal content – and by all means, are *not* sinful!

Tell her in *your* very own way, *"You're mine, for keeps!"*

iii.) Give genuine compliments:
Genuinely compliment the love of your life. Compliment her on everything; ranging from as noticeable as her newly washed and set hair, to something as intrinsically esthetic as her choicely taste of musical genre! Never allow that privilege to pass to another who gets to *notice* the improvements, *discovers* her likes and *offers* her compliments, before you!

Always claim the *top* position to acknowledge, honor and

shower her with genuine compliments! Be lavish with your praises.

When you verbalize genuine compliments addressed to your spouse, you demonstrate *your approval of, love and respect for her.* These in turn help notch higher, her self-confidence and morale! Self-confidence boost is to the females what ego-booster achievements are to the males. Think of it, no human "stiffens up as a board", before compliments emanating from a genuine heart – and an honest tongue!

iv.) Cultivate the gift of listening:
Every person *can* be a listener – if they wish! Listening – like communication – is an art. It needs to be cultivated, patiently!

Cultivate the habit of listening to your wife. By this, I mean that you *study* her communication styles, deliberately, purposefully, *listening to her heart* as her lips pour out onto you.

I always teach men to purpose on intent – with the help of their spouses – to "train" to be quiet, even when she may *not* feel like talking! Maintain quiet; "hold your tongue" from uttering *any* speech; first, for ten seconds, then twenty, then, upwards of one-hundred seconds. Use a stopwatch for the accuracy of timing, if you need to! (You may want to extend that training to three minutes, at once, as you witness improvements in your "listenability". This exercise, I must emphasize, is for men, only!)

The reason a woman shuts out her man from *her* 'communications' – but rather dialogs freely with a stranger cannot be far-fetched from *his* unresponsive, un-sympathetic ears, cold reactions or callous jokes made in reference to the very issues that deeply matter to *her* core being! Therefore, if he doesn't want to lose his wife, *a* husband must refrain from corruptible communication, that is, *"silly and corrupt talk, coarse jesting which are not fitting or becoming ..."*[13]

Affair-proof *your* marriage; listen to *your* wife, more – and *more!*

v.) *Observe romantic and affectionate moments with your queen:*

Intimacy comes *not* without a price tag attachment! Ask yourself: *"What makes me shy away from being intimate with my wife?"* You are not intimate with your wife, possibly because you are unwilling to detach the price tag!

If you're willing to be brave and do things slightly differently, then, kindly endeavor to carry out this simple task:

• Get a clean sheet of A4 paper or a diary. With a black pen in hand, proceed to identify, writing on that piece of writing pad, *your "Reasons for Having Not Been Romantic towards Wife"* in bullet points.

Be reasonable with your self-evaluation.

• Next, bring same evaluation sheet/diary recording to *the* dialog table – and in a congenial atmosphere of warmth and love, discuss with your spouse, bullet-point after point! Achieving this in itself is an integral start on the journey unto a stronger intimacy!

Be not timid to get intimate with your wife; she's been longing for you to make that first move.

If she's available at the moment, take this book to her and read her this portion, inquiring of my claims. If she's away, call or send her a text, a tweet or a *facebook* e-mail to confirm my "naïve" assumption!

Besides *intimacy*, every woman, by nature, craves for affection! *Tell me, dear sir, that you didn't know your wife craves your affection!*

Of course, *she does!*

That woman craves for your cuddle and touch. Hold her close, therefore; fondly, tenderly, and carefully. Ensure your hands are supple – and slow on her skin!

Generally, *every* woman loves to be touched by clean, supple, tender hands. This translates if your job involves, for instance, handling heavy-duty machineries with sooty engine oil or working in a motor-mechanic garage, rid both hands of black grease, first; wash and mildly perfume your body before embarking upon affectionate moments with her! Always remember, the female skin is highly sensitive, softer and much more tender than yours!

When you bring your face closer to hers in the heat of passion, please be mindful of the abrasive effects your facial hair stubs could have on hers. Some women love mustaches and side-burns, *some don't!* Some, the tickling, stubby, prickling sensations tiny unshaven beard-stubs on their men's faces produce; *others don't*. Make sure you inquire of her, her preference.

When it comes to having sex, a man *must* guard against rushing ahead and leaving his spouse behind – as if he were on a 'race for dear life.' Given, the male by nature reaches an orgasm quicker than the female, his penis becoming flaccid after a climax! At this point, he is described as having entered the *refractory period*. During the course of this rest-time, the male organ remains in a state of inaction until he regains another erection.

The duration of the refractory period in which the male organ rests before achieving another erection, varies from male to male – bearing in mind too, other potential factors as age and health variances. The older a man becomes, the longer it takes to attain and sustain an erection. Thus, the longer a man can withhold himself from achieving a sexual climax, the more intense and enjoyable his and her passionate moments become. Additionally, with a sustained, lengthy romance before coitus, a man may achieve enriched multiple orgasms – just like his female counterpart. Training and exercising the *pc muscles* in both male and female help delay orgasm!

The female on the other hand, takes a while longer to awaken to her man's sturdy efforts at arousing her sexuality. In other words, she dwells longer, on a *plateau stage* of arousal and excitement. This "plateau-*ing*" of arousal would gradually increase or decrease *if* the male continues or ceases foreplay, accordingly!

The husband must learn to deny and delay his sexual

fulfillment, for his wife's sake. He achieves this goal by extending foreplay and romance.

When a female is finally sexually aroused and ready, there are involuntary tell-tale signals she gives! "Sensitivity" on the part of the male would be a major requirement. If he isn't watchful enough, he may miss, entirely, her *ready signs*. It is only at this time, that he may attempt entry into her: she is engorged and well lubricated to receive him.

It should be plain sailing from here onwards!

If you're an impetuous male, I would strictly counsel that you specifically ask your wife, to educate you! Strip away, *all* inhibitions and shame!

Nothing is as displeasing to a wife as a 'piggy-grunt'; a sexually satisfied husband who only approaches her for sex in order to gratify himself alone! In all honesty, I should be happy to let *him* know that Christ is as much displeased with him as his wife – if not more! This kind of a man does *not* portray Christ-likeness, at all! The only message he successfully communicates is: *'I don't care!'*

A scenario such as this may finally push the wife to a frustration point that knows no return. Under the English law, such men have been sued for marital/ spousal rape. Apathy from husbands in *not* doing enough to help their wives attain somewhat fulfilling sexuality or the total absence of ethics and discrepancy in the bedroom department had caused – and still is at the root of much citing of "ir-reconcilable differences", in divorce courtrooms across the land!

Again, I implore you: *"Please do not abandon your wife on the plateau stage of lovemaking; she is your wife – and not a sex toy!"* Neither are you engaged in a competitive mountaineering expedition; so you can go *slow!* Sex with *the* one ordained for you should result in a mutual, symbiotic engagement. Endeavor *she* hits the big "O", too! Be healed from your selfishness – or dare I say, ignorance!

The United Kingdom's National Health Service (*N.H.S*) disclosed in a report made public in 2011, that 30% of all men in the *U.K* suffers from premature ejaculation – and some accompanying psychological issues including clear-cut impotence or erectile dysfunctions. These problems have far greater effects upon these men, their relationships and families, than could be perceived!

Most males who suffer sexual dysfunctions suffer in silence! Coupled with their emotional agonies, some, indeed, *do* suffer the tortuous tirade of insults railed upon them by their wives, partners or girlfriends. This is a grievous form of emotional abuse meted out to psychologically defenseless males who may be far too ashamed to admit such!

If you suffer from any of these issues, it is time to "speak up". The first person you "open up" to is your spouse or partner! Communicate with her, your *true* problems. You will be surprised to learn of some women's ignorance about what impact a man's sexual dysfunctions has on him!

With understanding, care and sympathy on both sides, you both can surely have an enjoyable sexual life, without resorting to separation or divorce! I would subsequently advise that you *both* consider seeking the help of a christian counselor – or professionals in the medical field. You are *not* too old to learn!

The summary of my message to you: *"Always romance your spouse!"* Notch up your *play* by mutually consented methods that will make her enjoy *you*. Engage the use of your imaginative powers, both!

vi.) Develop together spiritually:

Always pray together! Praying couples stay together. Read and study the Bible individually – and together as well! Share inspirations at the family altar. Attend church services together – and support each other's ministries and callings. Pour into each other, not just physical investments but spiritual investments, too.

vii.) Continue dating:

Dating should *not* stop because you are married. Continue planning dates and organizing getaways with the anticipation to nurture your mutual love.

Organize vacations and trips exclusively just for you *both* – excluding the kids! Employ the use of the best hands and hearts that you both agree upon to take the children in while "you develop the wings of romance."

viii.) If your wife initiates or demands sex:

If your wife initiates – or demands – sex, please oblige her 100%. Do *not* humiliate her. Readily avail her what rightfully belongs to her. Always remember that in Father God's equation, you no longer possess exclusively rights over *your* possessions any more than she does over what *used to be* solely, hers!

If you reject her advance(s), you run the risk of condemning her to self-guilt for offering, sending her subconscious mind a thought that she is undesirable or unwanted! Your signals may as well send her into the ready arms of another!

If you're ill-disposed to sex at the time of her request, be sure to communicate your state of being! (Re-read my counsel on *Becoming a Better Wife, point iv; page 136*).

ix.) *Encourage one another, every time!*

x.) *Forgive each other, more readily!*

xi.) *Exchange gifts:*
Buy each other gifts – and exchange gifts, often, *not* just only on anniversaries, but every time your heart remembers him/her. The cost of the gift is irrelevant; but please ensure it's "qualitative". Render your gift with a pure, sincere motive and *not* primarily as a bribe for what you aim to gain!

Love should be freely given – and freely celebrated!

It is my hope and prayer that your marriage is strengthened by the teachings and counsel printed on these pages!

Summary of Chapter 4

1.) Parents and guardians can *no longer* afford to abdicate parental/guardian responsibilities on issues of sex-education to the state, schools, Sunday schools – or indeed, their kids' peers on the playgrounds, nationwide. All hands must be on-deck to ensure we educate our children, appropriately, from the grassroots: the home!

2.) You have lost your authority as a parent when you have lost moral and ethical bearings!

3.) *"What's so wrong with sex, then?"* Absolutely nothing, if used within the sole confines, which the Creator-Father had designated it.

4.) *"Should migraine necessarily prevent a wife from having sex?"* No, not at all! Contrary to popular opinion, migraine should rather encourage a wife to pursue sex with her husband!

5.) *"Is masturbation a healthy habit?"* Since the scriptures are silent on this issue, I would deem it wise to hold my peace, too. (However, you may revert to the pages whereupon I have discussed the *pros* and *cons* of masturbation in order to decide, personally, your opinion).

6.) We can all become a better people, regardless of our circumstances disappointments or hurts suffered. Remember:

> *"Better individuals make a better community, a better community, a better people, a better people, a better citizenry, a better citizenry, a better world!"*

Recommended Reading

The following books *will* enhance your understanding; improve your relationships, love life, sex and sexuality. Do ask for them at any Christian bookshop – or place your order online:

1.) *Red Hot Monogamy, Making Your Marriage Sizzle by Bill & Pam Farrel; Harvest House Publishers, 2006.*

2.) *The Way To Love Your Wife; Creating Greater Love and Passion in the Bedroom by Dr. Clifford L. Penner & Joyce J. Penner; Tyndale House Publishers, 2007.*

3.) *52 Ways To Have Fun, Fantastic Sex, A Guidebook for Married Couples by Dr. Clifford L. Penner & Joyce J. Penner.*

4.) *The Gift of Sex by Dr. Clifford L. Penner & Joyce J. Penner.*

5.) *The Power of a Praying Husband by Stormie Omartian; Harvest House Publishers, Eugene, Oregon, 97402. U.S.A.*

6.) *The Power of a Praying Wife by Stormie Omartian; Harvest House Publishers, Eugene, Oregon, 97402. U.S.A.*

7.) *Loving Each Other by Leo Buscaglia; Winston, New York; Holt Rhineheart and Winston, 1984.*

8.) *The Art of Kissing by William Cane; New York: St. Martin's Press, 1991.*

9.) *Solomon on Sex by Joseph P. Dillow; Nashville: Thomas Nelson, 1977.*

10.) *Love for a Lifetime by James Dobson; Portland, Oregon, Multnomah, 1987.*

11.) *Getting the Love You Want: A Guide for Couples by Harville Hendrix; New York, Harper and Row, 1990.*

12.) *If Only He Knew What No Woman Can Resist by Gary Smalley, Zondervan Publishers, 1998.*

13.) *The Marriage You've Always Wanted by Dr. Gary Chapman; Moody Publishers, 2005.*

14.) *The 5 Love Languages: The Secrets to Love that Lasts series by Dr. Gary Chapman.*

'Cultivating the Habits of Thanksgiving and Gratitude' will awaken in you, that needful understanding that of all the gifs He has gifted humanity, thanksgiving and gratitude are the only dues requested of us by Father God!

Also, this chapter aims to show you that your "burden" is much "lighter", in comparison to someone else's – whilst hoping that this truth will birth within you the desire to become more grateful – thus unlocking even more miraculous doors unto you!

"In every thing give thanks: for this is the will of God in Christ Jesus concerning you."
1 Thessalonians 5:18

Chapter 5

Cultivating the Habits of Thanksgiving and Gratitude

"Through Him, therefore, let us constantly and at all times offer up to God a sacrifice of praise, which is the fruit of our lips that thankfully acknowledge and confess and glorify His name."

Hebrews 13:15; Amplified Version.

Thus far, I have discussed *'The Greatest Gift of All', 'The Gift of Restoration', 'The Gift of a True Friendship',* and *'The Gift of Sex and Sexuality.'* These are the more prominent of the innumerable gifts the Creator Father God has *gifted* us! Doubtless, there are thousands more!

Unlike these many other gifts, however; *thanksgiving and gratitude habits* are a gift *not* received, neither receivable by *any* man because they are *not* in the category of gifts the Father endowed humanity!

Thanksgiving and gratitude are a gift due to Father God from humans; yet, the majority of us continue to find it extremely difficult to redound the praises due to Him!

Why would this be?

This is because offering an acceptable thanksgiving to the Father entails, majorly, a spiritual activity that commences with an inherent discipline of the body, soul and spirit!

Gratitude

Two words *"grateful attitude"* when conjoined make one word *"gratitude"*. Thence, gratitude is *the* attitude of gratefulness. Because attitudes emanate from a person's reaction to external stimuli, thanksgiving in the midst of trying situations – like every other attitude – needs being cultivated; that is, *worked at!*

Ours is a generation that take gifts for granted – particularly the gifts of nature and the Spirit! We are the "entitlement mentality" generation. We feel, we deserve *everything* – and in fact, we feel like being owed all! We have imbibed a state of mind that expects to get things freely, without blinking an eye!

If I were to ask, for instance: *"Are you ever grateful for spring and summer?"*; you'd probably count off, on your fingertips, enumerating with a quick tongue what things you're grateful for! *"O.K.; what of winter?"* – and immediately, an *"attitude"* automatically pervades the air!

The Depth of Winter

Being warm blooded, many of us do *not* love the big winter freeze. Yet, there has been a lingering, "man-made freeze" in place now, for a while. Citizens of the "free enterprise world" have been experiencing the most devastating recession in recent times. This has led to a big "freeze" in the governmental, corporational and personal spendings of each of the countries and inhabitants of Europe, North America and the Far East, with the exception of China - and possibly Brazil.

Now, because the governments of the *G8* economies are adopting ever-stringent budget-cut policies aimed at recuperating their maladies such as massive unprecedented job and market-losses, home-foreclosures/re-possessions, the banking sector failures and citizens' bankruptcies; increased anxiety and stress levels in residents and an unprecedented level of fear in peoples' lives are the resultant effects of such drastic measures!

Even if your abode is farthest from those temperate lands, your *spend-ability* too could still experience a spluttering cough, if adequate care isn't taken!

Why?

Because there is a trickle-down, spiral effect spun into action by these world-giant economies, that may eventually become all too evident in weaker, ailing economies!

Amidst the doom and gloom, the sadness and melancholic chaotic despairing times, one question preoccupies my mind: *'What should the attitude of the Christ-follower be?'*

A sage, who lived life to the fullest despite many hardships, is worth hearing. He was Saint Paul, the apostle. Here are three powerful lines of his exact prescription to the Christ-follower in the midst of gloom and doom predictions. Says he:

"Rejoice evermore.

Pray without ceasing.

In everything give thanks: for this is the will of God in Christ Jesus concerning you."

1 Thessalonians 5:16-18

If you have commenced reading this book from this chapter, you may likely challenge me with a corny look in the corner of your eye: *"How dare you tell me what to do — after all; what else have I, to rejoice about?"*

If you are the one the Holy Spirit has identified, please continue reading; there is a specific message *just for you* on the next few pages!

Grateful for just Clean Water

Permit me to depart the shores of the freezing "doldrums" of *Western* economic depression, for the warmer latitudes. This time, to South Africa.

In February 2011, *Sammy Joseph Ministries* outreached that part of Capetown, far removed from the glitzy Waterfront/Central Business District scenery of this magnificent city! Blackisdorb, a deprived shantytown settlement was one of the regeneration settlement schemes proposed by the government, aimed at housing the homeless temporarily, until they were eventually absorbed into permanent housing schemes!

As you would imagine, settlements such as Blackisdorb were devoid of life's basic amenities. They were inhabited by *the broken*, *the battered* and *the abused* – who themselves were abusers of whatever chance and time availed them, on a daily basis!

This particular settlement had a highly mixed population of illegal migrants and displaced peoples from the war-torn neighboring countries of the Southern African region. Prostitutes and pimps, drug users and peddlers, the jobless and thieves – each group aimed at slipping through the net into the posh "Capetonian" scenery. Amidst the prevalent slack, lack and crime, there was however *never* a lack of spiritually hungry inquisitive souls of the young and the middle-aged who had set out to our evening outdoor rallies, to inquire about the way of the Lord. They had come in droves.

Witnessing the power of the Lord touch, save and heal these whom the society has rejected was an ecstatic sight. You could see a new *transfiguration*, literally, on those faces!

I had preached three nights in a row – and held four services between Friday and Sunday, combined. That had taken its toll on our team members as well as myself! We had "leaked" much virtue! Not being of a huge body frame at *five-feet-ten* and *eighty-one kilograms* wasn't virtuous; those daily outreaches in the enervating South African summer heat had left me famished! To replenish, I had requested some boxes of refreshing apple juice.

I have always loved a refreshing drink in apple and orange

juice, that is, if I didn't prefer above it, just ordinary clean water. That has been my "addictive" habit-prescription for a healthy drink-lifestyle, for many years! But this habit was about to be changed. After a gruesome schedule ministering, counseling, praying and visiting, the artificial sweeteners in the juice had left me thirstier. *'I would be better off on ordinary bottled spring water.'* So I *had* thought!

The carton of bottled water my indigenous hosts had placed at my disposal had *not* been from a natural spring source afterall as had been advertised on the label: the stinging bowel pains caused by diarrhea *had* certified that truth!

As my bowels rumbled uncontrollably, I crunched in pain and frequented the loo contained in the *en suite* wet room at the hotel room I had stayed. As I writhed in chronic pains, I became embittered against God. The next couple of days – or so, my attitudes exchanged modes from rock-solid onto a *yo-yo*, from the joy of seeing the converts come to Christ to sadness; exultation to complaining. I hurt, physically and emotionally. In the intervening time, I started counting off my fingertips reasons *why* I shouldn't have traveled out to Capetown, in the first instance – and yes, I *had* quite many a genuine reason! *How quickly we turn bitter, sullen and sour when situations don't go our way!*

The more I writhed in pain, and stooled; the more emaciated I became.

Now, before you arraign me before "the magistrates", allow me to ask you: *"Have you ever been sickly, felt abandoned – and ten thousand miles away from home?"*

The Importance of Introspection and Retrospection in Cultivating the Attitude of Thanksgiving

There is a pronounced difference between *gratitude* and *thanksgiving*. Gratitude is offered when we acknowledge the receipt of a gratuitous favor or deed. At such moments, our emotions brighten up. We become excited, elated – and happy!

Thanksgiving, however, is due to Father God when we *have not* received the thing we asked for, even in prayer – but rather, some sudden, unexpected circumstances of life turned against us like a ferocious, ill wind. At such adverse times, Father God says, *"Give me thanks, even amidst the adverse circumstances you may be undergoing!"* At such times, most of us find His *thanksgiving prescription,* one that is very bitter to ingest!

A twin companion-trainer-team that has done ever so well over the ages in preparing and ushering "restored mankind" into *thanksgiving mode* in the face of present calamity or trouble are *introspection* and *retrospection*.

Introspection is the process of a spiritual analysis of an inward self!

You see, from my experience in Capetown I related earlier, the more pain and hurt I felt, the more I whined and complained. The more I'd complained, the weaker and more pinned out I'd become.

Somewhere, in that cyclonic tumble-drier spin of diarrhea

and a potpourri of emotions, I started to realize how weak I was becoming; my breathing was now belabored and it seemed as if my rib-cage was about to collapse on my heart. For once, I realized I *may* have been walking through "the valley of the shadow of death."

I'd actually thought I was going to cross to the great beyond!

Not that I was scared of death – but somehow, *I wasn't just ready to die, anyway, until I have fully accomplished God's intents for me on this planet.* Suddenly, I remembered how much Jesus, loved me – and had laid down His own life for me. At that instant, I *had* thanked Him for His sacrifice!

So, I'd so quickly transitioned; I'd quit complaining.

Instead of complaining – and recruiting more reasons to complain, my mind started to *find* more reasons for which I could be grateful. And I soon found another!

I was *not* qualified for medical aid in this country – and the few hundred Sterling notes I had in possession had been handed over to the local church's leaders to be invested on ministry projects. That translated that I only possessed some substantially "loose change" from which I'd intended to give my offerings and bless other individuals!

I'd started to recall scriptures; scriptures where the Father assures me of His presence and divine health. These had flooded my spirit. As I laid on my back, eyes transfixed as if in a gaze on an imaginary trans-fixture on the white ceiling, my spirit had begun recounting the

Lord's blessings – including the comfort of His word in times like this!

As if obeying a divine command, the abdominal pains had ceased. *Abruptly!*

Diarrhea and dysentery – coupled with gastroenteritis – had killed many indigenes; what was so different about this fluffy Brit with no immunity, whatsoever? That fact had spun a new thread of thoughts within me, as I'd begun to *think!* And I'd thought some more. Like the shepherd boy David, in the wilderness, I *had* left my five children in a child-minder's care back home and had flown fifteen hours away; downwards, in obedience to *the* call! It had suddenly dawned on me that I *may* never have seen them again, without saying goodbye! That was a chilling thought – that had sparked a prayer!

Introspection had perfected its duty; it had guided me onwards onto positive reflection and meditation!

Friend, when you are in pain, discomfort or hardship, learn to revert your outlook, inside out! Look inwards. Self-examine. Soul-search. Search for just that *lone* reason for which you could be thankful!

> *"Examine and test and evaluate your own selves to see whether you are holding to your faith and showing the proper fruits of it. Test and prove yourselves [not Christ]. Do you not yourselves realize and know [thoroughly by an ever-increasing experience] that Jesus Christ is in you – unless you are [counterfeits] disapproved on trial and rejected?"*
> 2 Corinthians 13:5; Amplified Version.

Now, if introspection leads to reflection and meditation, retrospection is that teacher that aids the cultivation of the attitude of gratitude!

Daily issues will keep evolving aimed at making you become bitter, angry and resentful. If you negatively respond to *any* of these negative stimuli, you will soon find yourself enslaved, at will. You will suddenly discover that you've become a captive; ensnared, embittered and enraged with *everyone* – and *everything* you come in contact with!

Job loss?

Indebtedness?

House-foreclosure?

Redundancy at fifty-nine?

Pregnancy miscarriage or childlessness?

You probably crashed your spotless new car when an uninsured driver unexpectedly "cut in", in front of you; you've swerved to avoid them, to no avail. Your car emerged a total wreck! You got very angry and overwhelmed! There seems to be neither justification nor rationale at all, to be thankful!

You may have recently received bad news from your doctor following a medical examination: your health probably seems not to be on the mend! Your emotions suddenly become hollow; your entire life, suddenly caved in!

Maybe you were recently bereaved of a dear young one, in the prime of their life – and were left wondering 'why'?

*Should you be grateful to God **for** any of these painful unfortunate incidents?*

No, I would suppose, not; since He isn't the author of misfortunes! Indeed, there is absolutely nothing to be grateful for in evil occurrences!

*Should you be "thankful" to God **in** any of these painful unfortunate incidents?*

Yes!

Even though the Father *does* understand our human frailties; that we may *not* be able to switch, automatically to thanksgiving in hard times, nevertheless, as soon as we could open the door unto *introspection*, we would be in alignment with His divine will!

Not only this, but as soon as you *could* commence thanksgiving in the midst of *your* pain, inner healing commences. During this process of healing amidst the hurt and the pain, you must endeavor to follow through with the regime laid out by the "twin trainers." You would allow the processes of *introspection* guide you onwards onto *meditation*, which eventually places both your hands into those of *retrospection*.

It is after the expiration of the period of retrospection that you would see reason in St. Paul's admonition to give thanks unto the Father, *"in all things."*

Notice with me a few thoughts on *retrospection:*

- *Retrospective times are times designed for humans to pause in order that they may evaluate and weigh their gains against pains!*

- *Retrospective times are a moment of deep, spiritual reflection.*

- *The ability to arrive at a rational conclusion hallmarks the human heart from other primates'; 'retrospect' is that sole factor which enables that process.*

"Be thankful in all things," God's word teaches.[1]

Following your miraculous escape from that car crash that almost totally wrote you off with it, *retrospect* instructs of *your* need to be thankful for *the* miracle of your life's preservation! (Fortunately, too, you possessed a comprehensive insurance policy!)

Introspection precedes reflection. Reflection precedes meditation. Meditation engages *retrospection.* Suddenly, you quit focusing your energy and thoughts essentially on your loss; you utter a *word of gratitude* to the loving Heavenly Father, with respect to your gains even through that pain or loss!

The middle-aged person made redundant who initially couldn't sight a blurry star in a pitch dark sky suddenly *realized* that he/she lives in a country where employment laws are firm enough to ensure they get paid their entitlements/redundant package. That payment fortunately, amounts to a somewhat tangible sum! *Retrospection* resumed duty in their thoughts after they overheard in *SKY News at 9*, a highlight story of pensioners in some countries of the world who were owed their entitlements, for upwards of fifteen years into retirements/redundancies.

More, a new idea suddenly floodlit their mind. They implemented it – and it worked! They are back at work; self-employed and additionally, have become an employer of labor!

Whatever hard blow life has dealt you, I assuredly declare unto you that *if* you *would* allow both *introspection* and *retrospection* their due courses, you *should* soon find reasons for which you'd be grateful!

Now, "how long" could a normal retrospective reflection take?

That question I will answer in the next few paragraphs.

Honor the Throne

We have a unique heritage and culture in the United Kingdom of Great Britain & Ireland with respect to the monarch, Queen Elizabeth Windsor – popularly known as *the* Queen.

Queen Elizabeth is the longest ruling monarch. Our national anthem *"God Save the Queen"*, solely dedicated to the honor of Her Royal Majesty, petitions the Heavenly King:

> *"God save our gracious Queen / Long live our noble Queen / God save the Queen / Make her victorious / Happy and glorious / Long to reign over us / God save the Queen."*

Similarly, *every* currency in the United Kingdom – notes and coins – bear on its obverse side, an inscription of the thronehead, the Queen! All her subjects at home and overseas – in fifty-three Commonwealth nations of the world – accept with joy, their duty to honor Her Royal Majesty!

In an incomparable yet similar vein, shouldn't all earthly subjects of the Heavenly Kingdom more than rejoice and accept with an equivocal unanimity, their duty to honor HIS HEAVENLY ROYAL MAJESTY?

Now, *respect* and *honor* are two separate issues. For instance, an under-worker necessarily is duty-bound to respect the boss, by context of a mere, ordinary position he/she occupies. The respect such a subservient worker accords *the head* may be reprehensible, lacking honor!

Conversely, though, no person ever gave honor without paying a due respect – both in *context* and *content*. Children, for instance, honor their parents – even in their frail old years because they realize, they owe their very breath to them. Father God's children honor Him because they owe their *very* existence to Him!

> *"For in Him we live, and move, and have our being …"*
> Acts 17:28

When we cultivate – and exhibit – the ability to render

our gratitude and thanks to the heavenly Father despite the hardship we bear and the pain we suffer, we send a high, sonorous-pitched note to the opposer's camp, of our irrevocable honor to *His Heavenly Royal Highness!* Remember, we may not always know *why* certain events transpire in our lives; why a sunny day suddenly becomes overcast within hours – or indeed the reason(s) for which we must endure such tremendous pains! However, one thing is certain: we *do* know that our gratitude in the face of fortitude sends aching jabs to the devil's brain! This is why the invincible *Thronehead* of the invisible Heavenly Kingdom encourages us to develop the discipline and cultivate the habit of thanksgiving – not *for* all things, but *in* all things!

> *"In everything, give thanks, for this is the will of God in Christ Jesus, concerning you."*

How long should a retrospective reflection take?

Positive retrospective reflection should take as long as possible *until it has accomplished its assigned healing and growth roles on a person's inner being.* The "cultiva-bility" of *the* attitude of gratitude and thanksgiving in the midst of adversity earns Father God, the honor. It also yields a powerful avalanche of strength, healing and restorative miracles to the *payee* of such dignity! This right attitude towards God in his pain had turned the captivity of Mr. Job of Uz, captive!

Thanksgiving strengthens fortitude – past the mere ability of the human spirit in the day of grief! Woe betides that one lacking thanksgiving in the day of *the* refiner's furnace!

The Refiner's fire

Every manufacturer conducts controlled quality-control assessments on their artisanship; the more precious the craft, the fiercer the tests! Similarly, every fruitful citizen of the heavenly Kingdom will undergo the heavenly quality control monitoring!

Because fire purifies and reveals the quality of gold, the King chooses *His* fiery furnace as their *transient* abode during the testing!

There isn't anything to fear about this furnace, because like every goldsmith, He closely monitors and regulates the conditions therein! Moreover, the furnace-experience never lasts the jewel's lifetime; it is just for a *season of testing!*

Make no mistake about it; *you* will be tested!

> *"There hath no temptation taken you but such as is common to man: but God is faithful, who will not suffer you to be tempted above that ye are able; but will with the temptation also make a way to escape, that ye may be able to bear it."*
> 1 Corinthians 10:13

The question you ought to ask yourself, therefore, is this: *"How valuable am I to the Father King?"*

Your worth is unquantifiable! The Blood of God's Lamb already had that defined – if you are His! However, *His* furnace reveals your work's value: whether it is gold, silver, precious stones, wood, hay or stubble. *"Every man's work shall be made manifest: for the day shall declare it, because it shall be revealed by fire; and the fire shall try every man's work of what sort it is."²*

Your attitude and reactions of the heart in times of pressure and trials are a major criterion for determining your work's value!

Once available, *your* test-results upload "super-matically" onto *the King's Rewards & Awards Sheet,* from which rich eternal rewards, awards and golden incorruptible crowns are presented the King's *"true and faithful stewards".* The venue of this beautification ceremony had been eternally reserved for the *Beta Seat Judgment!³*

Isn't this a valid reason *why* you must endeavor to fulfill His purposes on the earth – and *not* your selfish, fruitless ambitions?

Father God has one sole aim in mind whenever He allows any of His children to undergo the refiner's fiery furnace: that they may come forth pure and luminous, as gold!⁴

Additionally, *Romans 8:28* implies that what life incidents were originally meant, fashioned and intended by the enemy of your soul to manipulate you out of joint; steal, maim, kill or destroy, God, *your* Throne-authority *will* work out for *your* eventual good!

The devil will attempt to restrict unrestrained, your vision and outlook on life. He will do everything in his power to make you hate on God – and the things of God. He will prefer that you'd rather be kept focused on the wrongs and the pains you've suffered. Satan, the evil one will do everything he possibly can, to foul your spirit. On various instances, he will squeeze a lemon juice in your mouth so that *your* spirit may become sour, curse God or preoccupy your mind from professing your loyalty and honor to the Throne Supreme. But *you* mustn't let him achieve his aim, any further than he already has! You have to purpose deep within, to re-commence offering unto God *"pleasing service and acceptable worship, with modesty and pious care and godly fear and awe."⁵*

You must learn – in the midst of life's crises – to say to the devil: *"No way, Satan, I owe my voluntary allegiance to the Supreme Heavenly Throne, no matter what. As long as I have my breath, I will praise my God!"*

When you begin to learn to speak in this manner, the devil learns to flee from you.⁶ When he flees, you will know it; you become emancipated – you experience supernatural deliverance in earthly realms!

Think of Job

Think of Brother Job of the Bible for a moment: the sudden inexplicable loss of his ten children – coupled with the whole farm estate in just a single day!

Rather than turn bitter, utter profanities, swear and curse the heavenly Thronehead as his wife had goaded him to do, before she'd walked out on him – all evidences of a dishonoring heart – Job did something drastic. While he still mourned in a despicable state of great body-anguish and brokenness of heart; he, in quick retrospect, *"worshipped God".⁷*

How could that be?

Job worshipped *the* Thronehead because he had a firm spiritual understanding of what honor means! This is the same understanding I entrust the Holy Spirit will help me pass onto you, today! Despite the decimation of his health and wealth, Job possessed *this* divine understanding that *if* only he would honor "He Who sits upon the Throne", he would encounter Him!

And he had! What an honorable man!

In all of his encounters with the forces of hell in the fiery furnace, "*Job did not sin with his lips.*"[8]

He held fast his integrity.

He did *not* dishonor God!

The first time I heard of the servant of God, Nick Vujicic, a man born without limbs, yet inspiring millions across the globe with his *'Life Without Limits'* message, I had a re-think! I kicked into retrospect, ever so suddenly!

The impact of Nick's message upon me was timeless. If you live in the West, I recommend you attend one of his crusades. If your abode is in the East/Far East, get hold of his DVD's. If you're from Australia, you already probably know of him as your compatriot – and if you reside in Africa, Central or South America, *Google* his name and watch clips of this immense man of depth freely, on *You-tube*. You may also log onto *www.lifewithoutlimbs.org* – your thinking will forever be positively enhanced, your gratitude tank, filled to the *very* brim.

Job, despite his agony – and amidst heavy sighs, breathed at his captor's face:

> *"I may not be privy to why things went drastically downhill, yet if I were to die in the midst of my affliction, I would still honor my Father, my King, unto death! He alone has my allegiance!"*
>
> Job 13:15; my rendition.

What a soul!

Master Jesus uttered a statement, comparable to Job's declaration:

> *"For whosoever will save his life shall lose it; but whosoever shall lose his life for my sake and the gospel's, the same shall save it."*
>
> Mark 8:35

Listen, if you want to preserve your life in the midst of the fiery furnace and amidst life's excruciating pains and pangs, you *must* begin today, to cultivate the attitude of thanksgiving. Jesus Christ the Lord gave thanks *in* all things; so should you! This is God's expectation of *you*.[9]

Two Reasons Why our Generation Will Remain Ungrateful

In closing, let me bring to your attention *just* two – among many – reasons why our generation will remain sullen, bitter and pitiable:

1.) The Presence of a Narcissistic, Self-pitying Culture:

Our adoring of a narcissistic, self-pitying culture that

has so readily found replacements for the worship of *the* true heavenly God in Hollywood and Entertainment stars, T.V. Talk-show hosts – and internet entertainment, in general, will *not* allow us to worship God in our pains! Subconsciously, our ears are attuned to these "idols" to such an extent that they rule over and guide our convictions. When trouble comes, we have found ourselves remembering their *"how to's"* formulae approaching the storms of life, in direct opposition to the panacea found in Father God's words, the Bible.

Sure enough, as we are bound to find out when we miss it, we turn inwards, self-pitied, sullen and sulky! We'd want no one to advise us on how to get back on the right track; this 'inward-looking' tendency soon tailspins into a lifestyle of self-pity and depression, the very neighbors of ingratitude!

2.) *Possessing a Wrong Yardstick of Success:*

Not only has our myopic-nature placed us at risk of ingratitude, our tendency adopting an unfavorable measuring yardstick of success, forces us to aspire and compete with other people whom we – alongside the society regard as successful. This has exposed us to a higher risk of independence away from the Divine One!

If we continue to demand for performance and the desire to outperform others, we will remain midgets in the understanding of the *only* gift it behooves us to offer the Father: *our* thanksgiving.

"They measuring themselves by themselves, and comparing themselves among themselves, are not wise."

2 Corinthians 10:12

Summary of Chapter 5

1.) Two words *"grateful attitude"* when conjoined make one word *"gratitude."* Thence, gratitude is *the* attitude of gratefulness.

2.) Because attitudes emanate from a person's reactions to external stimuli, thanksgiving in the midst of trying situations – like every other attitude – needs being cultivated; that is, *worked at!*

3.) Thanksgiving and gratitude are *a* gift due to Father God from humans; yet, the majority of us continue to find it extremely difficult to redound the praises due to Him!

4.) Painful situations in life would strongly contest with your emotions. Control your response to life's adverse stimuli engaging the use of *introspection* and *retrospection!*

5.) If you choose to respond to life's negative stimuli, negatively, you will soon find yourself enslaved, at will. You stand the robust chance of becoming a captive; ensnared, bitter and enraged with *everyone* – including *everything* you come in contact with!

6.) Developing an attitude of gratitude and thanksgiving in spite of the pain we undergo honors the One Who sits upon the Throne! It is our duty-call to *honor the Thronehead, always!*

7.) When we cultivate – and exhibit – the ability to

render our thanks to the heavenly Father despite the hardship we bear and the pain we suffer, we send a high, sonorous-pitched note to the opposer's camp, of our irrevocable honor to *His Heavenly Royal Highness!*

8.) *You* must learn – in the midst of life's crises – to say to the devil: *"No way, Satan, I owe my voluntary allegiance to the Supreme Heavenly Throne, no matter what. As long as I have my breath, I will praise my God!"*

9.) If you want to preserve your life in the midst of the fiery furnace and amidst life's excruciating pains and pangs, you *must* begin today, to cultivate the attitude of thanksgiving. Jesus Christ the Lord gave thanks *in* all things; so should you! This is God's expectation of *you!*

References

Chapter 1

[1.] Isaiah 21:4
[2.] Genesis 6:6-7; Amplified Version.
[3.] Genesis 1:28
[4.] John 10:10 refers to Jesus' description of the devil.
[5.] 1 Timothy 1:8-10
[6.] John 4:24
[7.] Galatians 3:13-14
[8.] Romans 8:28

Chapter 2

[1.] Hebrews 12:9
[2.] James 1:13-15
[3.] 2 Corinthians 5:17
[4.] Joel 2:25
[5.] Proverbs 3:8
[6.] Jeremiah 18:1-6
[7.] Ephesians 1:6
[8.] Revelation 5:12
[9.] James 1:17

Chapter 3

[1.] Hebrews 12:14
[2.] 2 Corinthians 7:10
[3.] Proverbs 13:20
[4.] Joshua 1:9-27
[5.] 1 Kings 12:1-14
[6.] Exodus 20:14
[7.] 2 Corinthians 6:14
[8.] 1 Corinthians 5:9
[9.] Proverbs 6:26
[10.] Romans 14:5
[11.] 1 Kings 13:1-24
[12.] Psalms 116:11
[13.] Jeremiah 8:22
[14.] Isaiah 7:14
[15.] Isaiah 9:6-7

Chapter 4

[1.] *www.essence.com/2010/04/21/trauma-sexual-abuse-monique*

[2.] *1 Peter 1:16*

[3.] *LBGT is an acronym for "Lesbians, Bisexuals, Gays & Transsexuals"*

[4.] *1 Thessalonians 4:3-8*

[5.] *1 Corinthians 6:19-20*

[6.] *Genesis 3:6*

[7.] *Hebrews 11:36-40*

[8.] *Romans 12:1-2*

[9.] *1 Corinthians 6:18-20*

[10.] *Ephesians 4:2; Amplified Version*

[11.] *Romans 13:1-3*

[12.] *Ephesians 4:15*

[13.] *Ephesians 5:4; Amplified version*

Chapter 5

[1.] *1 Thessalonians 5:18*

[2.] *1 Corinthians 3:12-15*

[3.] *2 Corinthians 5:10*

[4.] *Job 23:10; Amplified Version*

[5.] *Hebrews 12:28*

[6.] *James 4:7*

[7.] *Job 1:20-22*

[8.] *Job 2:10*

[9.] *1 Thessalonians 5:18*

Worship with Us

The Harvestways Int'l Church,
(Birmingham, U.K.)
Holloway Community Hall
Northfield, Birmingham,
England, United Kingdom
B31 1TT
Sundays: 12 noon–2pm
Fridays: 7–8.30pm
Tel: (+44) 7854675159
(+44) 7758195466

The Harvestways Int'l Church
(Nigeria, West Africa)
1 Harvest Way, Off Elewura Street
Behind Zartech / GLO Office,
Challenge G.P.O Box 2910
Dugbe, Ibadan Oyo State,
Nigeria, West Africa.
Sundays: 9am
Wednesdays: 6pm

You may want to inquire about SJM, invite Rev. Sammy to minister for
you or become a partner; please contact:
Sammy Joseph Ministries
P.O. Box 15129
Birmingham
West Midlands
England
B45 5DJ
Mobile: (+44) 7854675159
(+44) 7758195466

Other Books by the Author

Other books by the author are available at any Christian bookshop near you, Pulse Publishing House locations or from our website: *harvestways.org*

Destroying the Power of Delay: Possessing Your Canaan

This book is an expository piece of work, written in a scriptural, thought-provoking style. The author aimed at sharing with you from more than fifteen years of counseling in ministry, how to avoid the endearing long arms of delay; and if you're already entangled in a wild romance with the hated alien, the quickest way of escape from him.

Furthermore, real-life issues such as 'Causes of Delay', 'Who Should Care for the Elderly?', 'Wisdom Handling Inextricable Covenant Relationships', 'Liberating Financial Management and Dealing with Indebtedness' are adequately discussed. Others topics include: 'How to Effectively Handle Mid-life Crisis, Depression, Barrenness' - et cetera! (230 pages)

GIDEON: Releasing the Potentials Within You

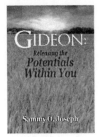

This book draws analogies from the life of Gideon (one of Israel's Judges) and applies them to how you can effectively release the hidden potentials within you. Written in easy, straightforward, simple language, you will find basic practical insights that will help lift you above common mediocrity levels in life! (188 pages)

Before You Step into Someone Else's Shoes

This book contains easy-to-do guides on how you will not repeat the costly mistakes made by others faced with a fresh opportunity to begin anew after suffering a heavy setback. We have also provided essential checklists to anyone willing to step into shoes ordained of God for them – as well as checkmating the mutineers! (46 pages)

Download *PULSE On-line*, freely at *www.harvestways.org*

Contact Addresses

United Kingdom
The Harvestways Int'l Church
@ Holloway Hall, Ley Hill
Birmingham
England
B31 1TT

or

Sammy Joseph Ministries
Box 15129
Birmingham,
England,
U.K
B45 5DJ
Tel: *(+44) 7854675159*
(+44) 7758195466

Nigeria
Pulse Publishing House
Plot 1, Harvest Way
Behind GLO Office
Challenge
G.P.O. Box 2910
Dugbe
Ibadan
Nigeria.

PULSE Publishing House also avails you a secure processing and prompt worldwide shipment of orders via harvestways.org, WHSmith.co.uk, Barnesandnoble.com & Amazon.com

Notes

CPSIA information can be obtained at www.ICGtesting.com
Printed in the USA
BVOW02s2253300315

393961BV00001B/25/P